Being
Better
THAN YOU
Believe

D1532472

Being Better

THAN YOU

Believe

8 Steps to Ultimate Success
Philip Berry

Outskirts Press, Inc.
Denver, Colorado

The opinions expressed in this manuscript are solely the opinions of the author and do not represent the opinions or thoughts of the publisher. The author has represented and warranted full ownership and/or legal right to publish all the materials in this book.

Being Better Than You Believe
8 Steps to Ultimate Success
All Rights Reserved.
Copyright © 2011 Philip Berry
V4.0

This book may not be reproduced, transmitted, or stored in whole or in part by any means, including graphic, electronic, or mechanical without the express written consent of the publisher except in the case of brief quotations embodied in critical articles and reviews.

Outskirts Press, Inc.
http://www.outskirtspress.com

PB ISBN: 978-1-4327-5636-9
HB ISBN: 978-1-4327-5642-0

Outskirts Press and the "OP" logo are trademarks belonging to Outskirts Press, Inc.

PRINTED IN THE UNITED STATES OF AMERICA

Table of Contents

Acknowledgements

The writing of this book has been a labor of love. It would not have been possible without the advice, input, and support of numerous people. I was inspired because, as I have worked with people throughout the years, many suggested I put my thoughts on paper. I would like to acknowledge some of these individuals and thank them for their contributions... Not in any particular order, except the first one.

This writing would not have been possible without the support, input, and wisdom of my wife, Karen, who has tolerated my long days, nights, and weekends working on this. She created the atmosphere that has enabled me to focus. On the important issues she made critical comments along the way to make sure that I am saying the right things, with the right perspective... I dedicate this book to the life we share together.

Thank you to my son, Kiel, who has also provided his very helpful perspective in marketing and finance. I appreciate him more and more each day.

Thank you to my daughter, Maya, who gave me rich examples and put a touch of reality to some of my thoughts. I am so grateful for her.

To Dolores Caldwell, who has been a mentor to me and who encouraged me to strive for change in my life. To Helen Hendricks, who knew me from way back when and so generously aided my growth. And to my good friends Richard Jones, Waldo Jeff, Jessie Combre, Steve Sims, Mario Reid, Seymour Hodge, Florence Ferguson and Debbie Williams, who have helped me grow and watched my personal changes. To my godfather Collins Reece and god brother Reuben Reece who have passed, but whose guidance still lives with me. To Donnie Johnson, whose homespun wisdom has made a difference in my life and aided my journey.

To my counselor Sarita Bhakuni, who nurtured the seed in my mind about writing this book.

To Richard Block, who sat with me over breakfast at the Waldorf a number of times and brainstormed the idea, which has become the title of this book. He is a change master, and I am grateful for his friendship.

To Jay Hershenson of City University, for his friendship, guidance and support through the years in all that I have tried to accomplish.

To my publicist team Amy Greenfield, Elizabeth Hershman, Karen Ash, and Alan Horowitz for their dedication and resources enabling me to make this dream a reality. I could not have done this without them. Alan's input was especially indispensable.

To Joe Maniscalco for his artistry in representing my thoughts in the cover design.

There are also many cheerleaders. Without their voices, this would have been difficult. Among those whose commentary I appreciate are Eugene Kelly and LH Whelchel. Simon T. Bailey, for his brilliance and advice on how to write a book: chapter by chapter so it doesn't seem too big!

To my sister, Elaine Habibah, for her support and encouragement.

To the numerous people who allowed me to use their experiences as examples. Your struggle is my struggle.

To the Creator, for all of the blessings I have received. Thank you for allowing me to be a vehicle to help others improve their lives and be better than they believe.

Introduction

Those who made a change

On the surface all was well with Mary. She was about 35 years old, worked for years at a federal government job in her hometown in the South. Her life was steady, predictable, and solid: a happy marriage, two wonderful children, a responsible and well-paying job, a nice house and plenty of material possessions. Everything needed to achieve the American Dream was hers, it seemed. But she was unhappy. A sense of dissatisfaction constantly nagged at her. She felt a bit like Charlie Brown of the Peanuts cartoon -- constantly walking around with a cloud over her head.

She came to me for assistance, and I helped her look at her life in ways that would reveal what was working well and what needed change. (I will go into considerably more detail later in this book as to how I help folks understand what makes them happy and what does not.) She thought about things she liked and didn't like. She paid attention to what bothered her and what made her happy. She assessed her skills to understand her strengths and their potential market value. She thought about where she lived -- the people, the community, and the opportunities -- and how well her living situation served her. She thought also about her family, to understand their role in her happiness and, perhaps, unhappiness. She considered what she wanted, what she had, and what she lacked. This took weeks and more than a little good-ol' soul searching.

But it all paid off. She learned a great deal about herself and her situation, and came to understand what was working well and what needed change. Her husband and children made her happy -- no problem there. But her job and hometown -- well, those were not addressing her needs. Where she lived was too limited and familiar.

She worked for the federal government, which was not the problem, but she had been at the same job for years and it no longer provided challenges, surprises, or creative opportunities. She was flying a straight, predictable course on automatic pilot, when she needed to be making some sharp turns and steep dives to test her limits.

From this analysis began a search that ended in Washington, D.C. She convinced her husband and children she needed a change. They realized they all could benefit from leaving their comfort zones and exploring new worlds. Her husband jumped at the opportunity; it turned out that he, too, felt stuck and wanted a change. Her children took more effort to convince, but when they learned about the opportunities they would have, they went from hesitant to excited.

For reasons of cultural, job, and other opportunities, she decided the northeast -- New York, Boston, Washington, or near these cities -- was where she wanted to live. Her need for a new job was easy to detect, but she did not know the type. So she started looking at many different job types and industries.

As it happened, she found a winner in Washington working for another department of the federal government: the same industry but a very different job. The new job and new city proved liberating. Her family is very happy. And so is she.

In the spring of one year, she could not imagine living anywhere but her hometown and working at the job she'd had for years. By the spring of the next year, she could not imagine why she stayed in her hometown and at her job for so long. Mary had a breakthrough when she decided to stop what she was doing, analyze her situation, and commit herself to take a chance and make a change -- a big change

Rob, who was in his 20's also made a major change. He lived what many would consider a charmed life. After graduating from a prestigious college, he immediately landed in the industry considered among the most glamorous at the time -- investment banking. Challenges, money, and even adventure were his, including a three-year company-paid stint in London, where he lived like a proverbial king. What more could someone in their 20's want?

As it turned out, Rob learned he wanted something very different. Like Mary, dissatisfaction dogged him. Assessing his situation, he discovered the job lacked independence and entrepreneurship, both of which he valued. Listing his strengths and weaknesses revealed that, for him, a much smaller organization where he could make a major contribution was more suitable to what he wanted in life than his current position of being a small spoke in a big wheel. The bottom line: goodbye to one of the world's most prestigious investment banking operations, and hello to a small but high energy boutique marketing firm, where he could use his financial skills to help this firm land contracts and grow its business.

Mary and Rob are now much happier. (I have changed their names and the names of most others in this book to protect their privacy.) Their choices surprised those who knew them -- and themselves. They took paths they never expected to be on. Their lives were controlled by what was expected of them; the benefits reaped were unfulfilling. Breakthroughs were needed to break out of their cycles of actions and reactions and to move in new, exciting, and challenging directions.

I call this book *Being Better than You Believe*, because in my decades of working with people, I have seen many like Mary and Rob change their lives in unexpected ways. They rid themselves of self-imposed shackles and find the freedom to pursue what is really important. They move to a new city, leave a prestigious job -- make major changes in their lives, the kind of changes most people are too afraid to attempt.

Rare is the person who lives to his or her full potential. Rare is the person who does not place self-imposed limits on what he or she can achieve. Rare is the person who does not undersell him- or herself. I will show you in this book a personal strategy that will enable you to manage your life and your career to their fullest, and make you better than you ever believed possible.

An irony I notice is that people often have strategies for the companies where they work -- detailed, well-designed, comprehensive strategies -- but lack a comprehensive strategy for themselves and their personal and professional lives. They work hard thinking through problems and challenges of their employers, but spend little time thinking through their own problems and challenges. They can quickly identify opportunities available to their employers -- new markets, new products, new services, and new marketing ideas -- but have no opportunities identified for themselves. This book provides the tools you need to assess your situation, understand your opportunities, and construct a strategy to maximize those opportunities -- to be better than you believe. What you may be doing for your employer, I will help you do for yourself.

Working to help you make a change

The consulting practice I run has a tagline that explains the goal of my work -- and the goal of this book -- "**being better than you believe.**" I used it for the title of this book because it captures what I am trying to achieve here. As I consult with and counsel others, many have asked for the formula to move forward with their lives. One size never fits all. No magic wand exists that can be waved and cure all your ills. Sorry to say, there is no magic formula.

However, if you follow certain thought processes that direct you to address certain questions; you can move a step closer to getting what you want. Our capacity to grow is greater than we imagine, but we don't always stretch ourselves to reach our fullest potential. Organizations often are constrained from accomplishing all they are able to because they don't tap into the creative reservoir of talent they have on their payroll and unleash those capabilities to the fullest extent possible. If we can get beyond the barriers and forces that constrain our thoughts and abilities, we can be better than we would have believed possible. In other words, we can do the impossible, though the "impossible" is actually quite possible, if we believe in ourselves.

Living up to one's potential has never been easy, but I would argue it has never in recent history been more important than it is now. We all face business and personal worlds changing faster and more dramatically than ever.

Consider what is happening in various industries. The American automobile industry is a shadow of its former self. The investment banking industry has reinvented itself in the past few years to remain relevant to the needs of the consumer in the 21st century. For years, the airline industry's profits have had the up-and-down frequency of planes taking off and landing. Media of all kinds (newspapers, television, and radio) are on the ropes, with futures that look troubling if not devastating. The department store industry holds a fraction of the retail market it had 25 years ago.

While these are "old economy"-type industries, the future of some of the "new economy" companies is constantly evolving. Twitter, Face book, LinkedIn and MySpace are moving the world of social media to a whole new level. I am sure there will be more to come.

In addition, employees in many industries face competition they never imagined they could possibly face -- from workers overseas. Much has been written about computer programmers and telemarketers who work for U.S. companies but live in India, Ireland, Indonesia, and elsewhere. But competitors in other industries are limiting the earning power of Americans. For instance, I've seen freelance writers in India and the Philippines bid on American writing projects posted on Internet job sites. And they expect pay of a few dollars an hour, less than any writer in the U.S. could afford to accept -- in fact, considerably less than the American minimum wage.

Americans are going to Singapore, Costa Rica, and other locales for medical and dental procedures, because good healthcare is available in many countries, often for a fraction of the price one pays in the U.S. How many writers or doctors who are, say, of Baby Boomer age, ever imagined they would directly compete with talented, trained writers and doctors in developing countries?

While the job scene is changing literally before our eyes, personal lives are also undergoing upheavals, though perhaps not as dramatically as in business. Being stuck in an unhappy marriage -- a common situation a generation or two ago -- now seems as though it was from another era. People today marry and divorce with greater frequency than ever.

Women have more earning power and more autonomy than at any time in modern history. Online dating sites now make it possible to "meet" potential mates anywhere in the country, even anywhere in the world. There are even online dating services for senior citizens. Moving from one city to another is easier than ever. Air travel is relatively inexpensive, and long distance telephone service is dirt-cheap, so children who move because of a parent's job change can now stay in touch with their old buddies to a degree never before possible. This makes it easier for parents to pick up and move the whole family.

Bottom line: Choices are greater today than ever before, opportunities are greater today than ever before, and the risks today of staying put --, as a result, greater than ever. Those who do the same thing over and over are the people who will never be better than they believe. In fact, they will never be nearly as good as they can be.

While the primary focus of this book is on personal change, organizations also need to consider how they will change in order to be more effective and productive. The principles I will talk about will give you insights into how to begin rethinking your organization's purpose. Whether you work for a corporation or not-for-profit, it is critical to think about how you can improve your business proposition. I will show you how these concepts apply to organizations looking to improve their ability to be relevant to their clients, customers, and employees.

This book will provide tools that will help you reach your potential, enabling you to have a breakthrough in your thought process. To put it in today's vernacular, you will be able to re-think your value proposition to your employer, life partner, or whomever, and reposition yourself. Perhaps you have been working in technical positions; a breakthrough might direct you to rethink your contribution to an employer and reposition yourself as a marketing person with technical expertise.

The purpose of this book is to stimulate your thought processes, to have you consider your present situation in a very different way. I want you to evaluate whether you are consciously doing the best that you can do -- for yourself or your organization. I want you to consider that embracing change can be more fulfilling than the status quo.

What I will help you avoid in this book is going around in circles, never quite breaking out of your established patterns. You can never be better than you believe if you keep doing the same thing over and over. In computer logic, there is a "do loop," which keeps repeating itself until it is true. In human experience, repeating oneself endlessly typically results in ending up just where one started. If you are happy with where you are, then you have no compelling reason to read this book. But if you feel you can do more and have more, then likely you are not being better than you can be, let alone better than you believe.

Keep in mind that because of advances to medicine and

nutrition, you will likely live longer than most did in previous generations. Baby Boomers, for example, will live more years in retirement than their parents or grandparents (though not as long as their children). They need to think about how they will be satisfied and fulfilled during the remainder of their lives.

But even younger people have to be dexterous and responsive. As I write this, it is tough for young people to find a job, any job. Opportunities, at least for the time being, are constricted, and young people need to adapt to this reality.

Both young and older folks have to assess their skill sets, review their capabilities, and consider their desires and goals, and place these within the context of industries likely to do well in the coming years. Previous career assumptions probably will not hold for any length of time.

My goal with this book is to have you reach beyond anything you ever imagined. I want you to make the changes that will position you to be everything you ever imagined and hoped for -- and more -- and not be stuck doing the tried-and-true, which has been so unsatisfying. When you have completed the process, you will be a different person than you are today, in ways like Mary and Rob. They changed significantly, and so can you.

The book's organization

I have arranged this book according to eight guiding principles, and devote a chapter to each. Note that each chapter starts with a quote. I have a fondness for quotes, which I have collected for years. Many are entertaining, while others are truly insightful. But the most important reason I collect them is because they can help focus my thinking, help position my thoughts around a core idea.

A favorite example is from a man who, though dead for over half a century, seems ever more popular, Albert Einstein: "Insanity is doing the same thing over and over and expecting a different result." To connect this quote more directly with this book, let me paraphrase it: You cannot get out of your rut and become better than you believe, by doing and thinking in the same ways you did that got you in the rut to begin with. At the end of each chapter are some questions, which I call thought stimulators. I encourage you to consider these as you think through how to make the principles applicable to you in your life and organization.

To be better than you believe requires a strategy, which is what I present here. The strategy's eight steps will take you from where you are now to where you want to be. This is a journey, and these principles are the trail markers that will guide your trip so you can achieve major breakthroughs in your life.

The eight principles are:

1. Why change?

2. Thinking differently

3. Anchoring your values

4. Creating the vision

5. Discovering your distinctive competencies

6. Change your paradigm and rebrand yourself

7. Networking and maintaining your personal board of directors

8. Creating opportunities for success

When beginning a journey, it helps to know where one is going and how one will get there. You are just starting this book, so let me now briefly describe each of these principles. Then, in subsequent chapters, you will read in depth about each and learn how to use them in your own life. Each principle builds on the previous one. Thus you can use this as a model for personal and organizational change. At the end I have a chapter called "Basking in the Glow". This chapter outlines some of the characteristics of those who have been successful in accomplishing their goals and achieving success.

1. *Why change?*

On the journey to breakthroughs and change, the first step is to understand why you need to change, or even if you need to change. Given the fact that you are reading this book strongly suggests you think change is needed. This first chapter will help you decide if you need to change, and why such change can bring more benefits and joy than you ever imagined.

2. Thinking differently

Once you decide change is needed, your next step is to start thinking differently. I will go into this in more detail later, but keep in mind a comment made by Norman Vincent Peale, the well-known proponent of positive thinking: "Change your thoughts and you change your world."

3. Anchoring your values

When people start to change their thinking, they begin to explore their values with an eye towards, perhaps, altering some of their values. Values guide our behavior and, in a sense, dictate the choices we make. Knowing and understanding our personal values is an absolutely critical component when we are hoping to change and make a major breakthrough.

4. Creating the vision

A powerful tool to help you change is visioning. With it, you can begin not just to think in new ways, but *see yourself* in new ways. With visioning, you can begin to dream how your life will be, and then be able to live that life.

5. Discovering your distinctive competencies

When you visualize yourself after you have completed this journey, you will have focused not just on what you want to achieve, but what you are able to achieve. Picturing yourself a concert pianist, though you have little in the way of musical talent, is not productive. Understanding your strengths -- the things you are good at and that most people are not -- is productive. I call these distinctive competencies, and identifying and capitalizing on them is essential if you are to be better than you believe.

6. *Change your paradigm and rebrand yourself*

Changing yourself internally is not enough. You need to change your image to the outside world so it sees you as you want to be seen. If you want to start a clothing store for fashion conscious businesswomen, do not dress in jeans and chew gum, even if this has been your usual course of behavior. This chapter discusses techniques you can use to change your paradigm and rebrand yourself.

7. *Your personal board of directors*

To change your paradigm and rebrand yourself requires the support of others. You cannot get where you want to go alone. You need to develop relationships that help you define your brand and sustain it, the subject of this chapter.

8. *Creating opportunities for success*

I do not believe in relying on luck. In fact, luck is a word I do not like to use. Life presents opportunities to virtually all of us. Those who have "luck" are really those who have prepared themselves with education, skills, experience, and attitude to have the willingness and ability to take advantage of life's opportunities. Here I discuss how you, too, can create your own opportunities for success and take full advantage of them.

Chapter 1
Why Change?

"Not everything that is faced can be changed,
but nothing can be changed until it is faced."

James Baldwin

Often, people think they need change when feeling some-how trapped, distracted, unsatisfied. It is as though an ill-de-fined wall stands between them and what they want to achieve. The sensation is frequently more felt than understood, but it is there. It follows them around and cannot be shrugged off. These folks feel a need to do things differently, but are not sure what the problem is, nor what to do about it. This can apply to relationships as well as jobs.

Whether you fully understand the source of your dissat-isfaction, or are still working to comprehend it, the road to becoming better than you believe starts with a very specific first step: the decision to change and not stay trapped in the status quo.

Why change? Consider:

Why are you here?

This is the perennial question some of us ask ourselves, while others completely ignore it. Why are we here? What is our purpose? What effect are we having on the world? How do we positively affect others -- family, friends, colleagues, even strangers?

This is a basic question, yet many of us, even after asking ourselves this for years, fail to devise a compelling answer. My purpose here is not to get into a deep philosophical discussion about the meaning of life, but to point out that how you view your purpose here on earth is a valuable brick in building the foundation you will need to reach your potential.

Do not be like Betty, whom I knew for many years. When close to death, she decided to write her obituary, an act that caused her to realize she had not thought much about her life's purpose. She told me she wished she had given it more thought years before, rather than now when she had little time to reflect on her life and no time to change the course of it. In fact, she admitted she probably would have done some things differently had she addressed this question years earlier.

Do not place yourself in this position. An exercise I often recommend to my clients is: If an obituary were written about you today, what would it say? Individuals need to think way in advance about what their obituary will say. How satisfied would you be with what your obituary had to say about you? If you would be unsatisfied, you need to change. We take a lot for granted in our lives. We assume tomorrow will come. We assume things will continue the way they always have. When we get to a certain point of comfort in life, we don't want it to change. This is a very natural reaction. After all, many of us have worked very hard to get to a certain level of comfort and when we reach it, we seek stability.

The issue is that we often get to a point when we ask ourselves if this is all there is. We question whether we are on the right path. We begin to seek answers to the gnawing question regarding our purpose. If you aren't feeling this burning desire to seek these answers, then you should put the book down now. If you feel that you already have it all figured out, then you are in a great place indeed. However, I would ask you this question: Are you indeed living to your highest potential? Are you willing to engage in an exercise that might uncover new horizons?

If your business is successful, then perhaps you don't have to even think about doing anything differently. But ask yourself, "What does success mean"? If you are making X-amount of revenue, sales, or profit, is that success? If you stay at that same level next year, would you still consider it to be successful?

How will you play the *"back nine"* of your life?

If you are not a golfer, pardon my golf analogy, but what

applies to virtually any sport -- football, tennis, basketball, golf -- applies to life as well: How are you going to live the second half of your life? Is it in line with how you envision yourself? Will you just amble through the second half, get by and eventually come to the final hole, or will you have a renewed purpose, a new direction? Will you play the back nine better than the front nine?

It is never too late to get a new sense of purpose and direction, though, of course, the sooner you do so, the better off you will be. The second half can, to use a cliché, be the better half. But you have to plan and work toward that end because it is unlikely to happen on its own. The second half of your life is not something you want to leave to chance.

Consider the career of Joy Behar. She went to Queens College for her Bachelors degree and received a Masters degree from The State University of New York at Stony Brook in English Education. For several years she worked as a teacher in the public schools system of New York. She married and had a daughter. However, things changed. Joy had an ectopic pregnancy and nearly died. Also her marriage was no longer working. These were life-changing events and she knew she needed a change. She was wondering if she was indeed working towards her dreams and decided to quit her job as a teacher and pursue a career as a comedian, which was something she always wanted to do.

She went to work as a receptionist at one of the major television stations and performed comedy routines in nightclubs.

She knew that there was more to life than what she was doing and wanted to pursue a new path in the back nine of her life. When she started down this new path she was 40 years old, but she didn't let that deter her from reaching her dreams. Today, Joy is a regular commentator on a popular talk show and also hosts her own television show. She also is in a very satisfying, long-term relationship with a man whom she calls her "spousal equivalent." She couldn't be happier with her new career because it is more in line with her passions, interests and values.

Reversing the Toilet Assumption.

The Toilet Assumption is a term developed by Philip Slater about three decades ago in his book, *The Pursuit of Loneliness.* He noted: "One begins to feel that there is a severe gap between the fantasies we live by and the reality we live in. We know at any early age how we are supposed to look when happy, and what we are supposed to buy to be happy, but for some reason ,our fantasies are unrealizable and we are disappointed and bitter. Once something is out of sight, it is out of mind." Put another way, individuals as well as society, when faced with difficult social problems, often flush them out of sight. And once out of sight, they fall off our radar screen and are out of mind.

The Toilet Assumption tells us we do not always face up to life's difficulties. Our actions prevent us from living in a way that meets our needs, but rather than change how we live, we flush the problem out of sight and refuse to deal with it. We create our own reality, but it is a false reality, a fantasy world.

Rachel was married fifteen years when she suspected that her husband was cheating on her. Actually, years earlier she had a strong feeling that he was cheating, but she could not accept this fact. She ignored many of the signals and refused to face the facts. He would work on irregular shifts and many times on weekends.

This went on for years, until Rachel learned from a very good friend that her suspicions were true and that her husband had a long term relationship with another female. In fact, for years, friends of Rachel hinted to her that her husband was cheating, but she would deny it. Ultimately the facts were so compelling that she couldn't ignore it any longer. She had used the Toilet Assumption for as long as she could to avoid facing a difficult situation.

Larry worked for 10 years at a media organization, where he was continually praised and told he was a good worker. During this time, he had three bosses, but never got the chance to move into his boss's position. True, he lacked a Master's degree like some of his supervisors, but he had considerably more experience than any of them and was good at what he did. The company needed him in his position, so it never offered him a chance to advance, though he made clear he wanted to move up.

For years, he believed he would be given the opportunity to become a supervisor, and he ignored all the signs he was not going to get that chance. He was paid well for his position, but this was a strategy by the employer to keep him content in his current position. Eventually, he took action by accepting a job with a company that valued his experience. This new employer accepted that he lacked an advanced degree, which was one of the traditional requirements for the job, but recognized he was better at dealing with detail than many younger people with graduate degrees. In fact, he did not appreciate how much he knew until he went on the job interview for this new position and was asked lots of detailed questions he was easily and quickly able to answer.

Today, he's a supervisor and much happier at work than he ever was at his former place of employment. He trains and motivates subordinates, is an effective leader and his department performs well. The Toilet Assumption held him back for about a decade, but eventually he accepted the truth and, when he did, moved on to a life of considerable professional success.

**People need to leave the fantasy world
behind and rewrite their life script.**

There's a phrase from *Alice in Wonderland* that's worth noting: "If I had a world of my own, everything would be nonsense... nothing would be what it is, because everything would be what it isn't."

Many feel that change is discretionary, something we can do or not do, depending on our desires. Alice's comment epitomizes this thought. Yet, many people need to rewrite their life script as opposed to living in the world of Alice in Wonderland. It is the difference between proactive and reactive. In my experience, many live in a fantasy world, constructing an alternative reality and, to justify that world, create rationales. These rationales determine exactly what they are supposed to do and how they will go about living their lives.

This is acting much like Alice, in that Alice creates her own world based on her view of how she imagines the world operates. We often create our sense of things. The world Alice creates may have been nonsense, while our worlds are, perhaps, more rooted in reality, but in truth, fiction is found in all our personal worlds. How we view things may not make "sense" to others, but makes sense to us.

The significance of these personal worlds is that they, to varying degrees, influence how we act. These worlds let us know how things "should" be, and how we are supposed to be and supposed to act. Problems develop when these fantasy worlds become controlling. Then we need to rewrite the script.

Ask yourself: Is the life I am now living the best life possible for me? Can I get more if I do something differently? What changes would I have to make for that happen? Is this the best performance my organization can deliver? What can I do to improve my products or services? Are there other markets I haven't thought about that can be serviced?

I am not suggesting everything you do needs change, but

I am suggesting that you continually examine what you do. Think of it as similar to continuous improvement in business, where a company has to constantly look for ways to improve its processes. Both companies and people never reach a final destination. Instead, they are always on a quest to make things better, even if the improvements are just incremental. View self-improvement as an ongoing journey, not a place you reach and never leave. Find those things in your life which seem immovable but which really deserve reexamination. Those are the aspects of your life you may need to change.

Change is a scientific necessity.

The scientific field of quantum physics has a word worth noting: entropy. It means all organisms move toward disorganization and death, whether a plant, a planet, a person, or an organization. To reverse the entropic process requires negative entropy. This requires bringing new thoughts, new ideas, new information, new resources, and new ways of proceeding. As a living organism, we can change our present state and move to a different reality.

Consider various industries. We all have heard about the buggy whip and horse carriage makers who are no longer with us because automobiles made them obsolete. Once, there were thriving ice making companies that would harvest ice, deliver it to customers' houses and put it in their iceboxes. This worked well until effective and efficient refrigeration for the home was developed, which enabled refrigerators to produce ice on the spot, making obsolete hundreds of large and small ice-making companies. More recently, similar turmoil has hit media, music, travel agency, and other industries. Companies in these industries will have to change or risk becoming the next buggy whip producers, horse carriage manufacturers, or ice makers.

As a society, we need to consider our education system. Thirty years ago, according to the International Scientific Board, the U.S. ranked Number 3 among all countries for producing scientists and engineers. Today we are Number 17. Asia produces eight times as many engineers as the U.S., for example. Given our approach to education, we will be competitively at a disadvantage in science unless we change. And this is at a time when science is more important in many economic sectors than ever before, including health, technology, and transportation. What will be the role of secondary learning institutions and colleges if we don't change our outlook?

What is success?

This brings me to another point: What is success? How do you, as an individual, judge success? The standard we use as individuals and as a society needs to be reexamined, which provides an opportunity for us to change the way we approach our lives.

Let me give you an example: healthcare. We have access to more processed fast foods, which are high in fat, low in fiber and contain refined sugars, than ever before. As a result, many of us eat more of these types of food than ever before. No surprise, then, that we are gaining weight. This in turn boosts the incidence of heart and other diseases. Our very success works against us.

Some feel the best gauge for success is how many possessions they have -- houses, cars, electronic toys. A bumper sticker I once saw said, "The best things in life are not things." We need to live more simply. This is not a new idea. In the 1970s, E.F. Schumacher had a best seller, *Small is Beautiful: Economics as if People Mattered,* which extolled this lifestyle. He highlighted the tendency of Americans to think big is better, that amassing more is desirable. Our houses have gotten bigger (I have read that today, the average American house is double the size of the average house in the 1950s -- even though families have gotten smaller), cars are bigger and fancier, as are televisions. We have more "toys," more things, more stuff.

We measure success by the quantity and quality of our stuff. Schumacher talked about our being bombarded by images of success on television: If you live in this neighborhood, wear certain designer clothes, frequent certain restaurants, you are judged successful. Then he pointed out another model of success. One based on the principle that less is more. In *Walden Pond,* Henry David Thoreau created a quieter, more reserved and contemplative life. It included fewer things, but a greater appreciation of what the world presents to us for free, such as nature's beauty. Many today are receptive to such thinking. Rather than going on fancy vacations, they stay home and make day trips in what are called "staycations." The slow food movement is another example. This all is part of a different model for living, a different model for success.

Perhaps it is time for you to examine your need for more possessions as a way to achieve happiness and success. Ask yourself: Are the trappings of success making me happy? How can I be happier and "more successful"? This has to do with reexamining your whole life's purpose, and being more proactive and more in control. With more control, we become originators and switch from passive to active. We originate the way our lives play out, rather than letting things happen to us. This start of this process can come from a phrase from poet and autobiographer Maya Angelou: "If you don't like something, change it, and if you can't change it, change your attitude."

Change cannot be approached until we: 1. look at our thinking process and how we are handling our life at this particular point, and 2. understand our thinking and work to change the thinking that is holding us back.

Organizations need to also continually reevaluate what success means. Is it success to reach a given level of sales and profit? Will this same level be successful in the next year or next three years? Of course not! Are sales and profit the sole indicator of what it means to be successful? It is certainly true that these are important indicators; however, now shareholders are asking companies to also show how they are being socially responsible.

For example, it is not uncommon for shareholders to want to know whether certain products are polluting streams, or whether the products have chemicals or ingredients which are injurious to people and the environment. Companies now need to be sure that they are not hiring underage children in their overseas operations also. Furthermore, they need to consider that the working environment for their employees is safe, as well as productive.

There are more women in the workforce, and the population of many countries, particularly the U.S., is becoming more diverse. In fact, the so called minority populations of the U.S. will be larger than the white population in 40 years. Throughout the world, different countries are facing other demographic shifts. These factors cause organizations to review their hiring policies and their policies to develop and retain talent. Success for corporations cannot be narrowly defined as annual increases in sales and profits anymore. Consumer groups, advocacy groups, and their customers now hold companies to a much higher standard.

What makes you successful today will not hold true forever. The paradox of change is that it is constantly occurring. If you stand still, in your values, thoughts, behaviors, programs, and actions, you will not be successful. In fact, it is difficult even to survive at the same level. Hence the theorem of quantum physics is realized. Organizations that do not take in new inputs will move to disorganization or death.

Change is the New Constant.

Many of us do not appreciate the changes that have occurred in our lifetimes. The changes of the last 100 or 200 years are obvious to everyone with some knowledge of history. Less obvious are the changes in our lifetimes, such as in the past 30 or 40 years. Technological change, particularly in terms of computers and the Internet, is readily evident, but many changes around us are more subtle and incremental, and therefore not as noticeable, though still significant. In fact, I would argue such changes are very significant, and probably affect our lives far more than we realize. The societal changes going on practically force us to make changes in our lives.

Which is why I often tell my clients: Change is the new constant. People used the same cooking techniques for hundreds of years. Today, people cook differently than they did even five years ago, and dramatically differently than 25 years ago. The microwave has brought a whole new dimension to convenience. Especially if you have school age children! Who heard of broccoli rabe or panko a few years ago? And 25 years ago in the U.S., who ordered all the different types of coffees that we now have at our disposal? It was just regular or black with cream or sugar. What was exotic is today found in almost every neighborhood supermarket.

Change is a constant in many other areas of our lives, as well. Communications (smart phones like the iPhone and BlackBerry), technology (such as the GPS -- global positioning system), and music (downloading music rather than buying it on a disc or tape) are a few of the examples of how change in this decade has played out.

Some changes are so subtle we don't realize they are occurring. In 1970, Alvin Toffler made his name as a futurist with his book, *Future Shock*. Ten years later, he wrote *The Third Wave*. In this book, he described the first wave as agrarian cultures, which replaced hunter-gatherer societies. The second wave was the Industrial Revolution, and was characterized by the nuclear family, industrial production, corporations and the like. The third wave, which began in the mid-1900s and continues to this day, is postindustrial. It is technologically driven, knowledge based, and decentralized. An example would be the move from mass communications toward more focused, niche-oriented communications.

Let me discuss our age of change in more concrete terms. Let's compare 1968 to 2008. I choose 1968 because that seems to me a watershed year, when a shift occurred among Americans against the Vietnam War, when the Reverend Dr. Martin Luther King and Senator Robert Kennedy were killed, when rock-and-roll hit a high point of creativity, when President Richard Nixon was elected and began a change in the country's political trajectory from more liberal predecessors, when the U.S. and other countries (France, for example) underwent dramatic turmoil and when the Baby Boomers started coming of age. I have noticed, myself included, that many people refer back to that year when making comparisons to the present.

It's easy for us to understand how change is occurring on

an intellectual level when we look over large bands of time, such as 60- to 100-year time spans. Shorter time spans, say from 1968 to 2008, produce more subtle but still very significant changes.

Television

Communications is an area that has undergone enormous changes. In 1968, television sported fewer than 10 channels; today there are probably more than 500. Cable television was just beginning, and was used primarily in places such as Manhattan where television sets had difficulty receiving over-the-air programming. Today, cable television has more prominence than the broadcast networks, as seen in the wealth of programs cable produces and the broad range of advertisers it attracts. Consider how many options you have to purchase cable programs. The astounding number of choices at your disposal is overwhelming for some.

Telephone

Television is not the only communication medium to experience profound change in just the past 40 years. Consider the telephone. Then there was one big telephone company -- AT&T. Now there are many phone companies -- AT&T, Verizon, T-Mobile, Sprint, Skype and others. Furthermore, you can buy phone service from cable television companies.

Those of a certain age probably remember when not only

did the telephone service come exclusively from AT&T (or Ma Bell, as we used to call it), but so did the phones themselves. Phone stores that now exist in nearly every strip mall were nonexistent. Furthermore the technology has changed. The idea of portable phones was the stuff of science fiction and newspaper comics like Dick Tracy and his telephone watch. That so many of us would be walking down the street, chatting on a phone, never occurred to most of us. Through the use of remote ear phones, it seems as if people are now talking to themselves.

This degree of change, as great as it is in the U.S., has been even greater in other countries. The U.S., in fact, does not have the most cell phone users. That distinction belongs to China, which in 1968 was undergoing the political upheaval known as the Cultural Revolution. Today it is an increasingly modern, internationally important power. India is another example of a country whose potential was underestimated in 1968, and now has more cell phone users than the U.S. That countries like China and India (and others such as Korea and Taiwan) would in some ways be as technologically advanced as the U.S., if not more so, was inconceivable 40 years ago.

An interesting aspect of change regarding the telephone is that mobile phones, unheard of in 1968, are overtaking land-line phones, the mainstay of the telephone market for over a century. In South Africa, for example, 41 percent of the population uses cell phones -- nearly twice the 22 percent using landlines. Not only has the usage of cell phones given individuals a way to instantly communicate wherever they are, it also expands the type of information they get.

Telephones aren't what they used to be. In fact, huge changes have really come about just since 2000. Moving from analog to digital, cell phones became personal devices that provide a wide arrange of services -- music, photographs, e-mail, Internet surfing, texting ("texting" wasn't even a word a short time ago) and, of course, verbal communication. Most Millenials, i.e. 18 to 25 year olds, use their phones more for sending text messages than making phone calls. Who imagined even 10 years ago that we would be using our telephones as cameras, or as devices that we typed into as well as spoke into? How people communicate, especially younger people, has changed dramatically. Face book and Twitter, to name two, have profoundly changed how people provide information to others. The level and degree of interaction has definitely been impacted with new technology in this area. Many people no longer rely on just face to face communication to interact about the most intimate aspects of their life.

Music

Sam Cooke, the great R&B singer, sang a song called "A Change is Gonna Come." He was never more correct, especially in the music world. In the past 40 years, we have gone from staid, safe American Bandstand, to the out-there, sometimes controversial American Idol. People had no immediate voice regarding what was popular and what was not. Only through record sales could they vote for their favorite performers and songs. Now, popularity is shown not just by purchases, but by actual voting. People vote for their favorite singers on such programs as American Idol, moving the public's involvement with music from passive to much more proactive.

In just this decade, with the introduction of Apple's iPod, as well as the availability of legal and illegal downloads from the Internet, the music industry has been turned on its collective head. Major retailers like Tower Records and Virgin Megastore, have closed their stores. Instead, people get their music from downloads. And they learn about bands from the Internet, rather than the radio.

The choices available for listening to music are far greater than ever. Hundreds, maybe thousands, of radio stations are available free via the Internet. Satellite radio offers dozens of programming options, just as cable television does for television viewers.

Reading

When I was younger, I went to the library, took out a book, read it and then returned it after a few weeks. All through my college education, I went to the library to research and study. If I didn't get there before it closed, I was out of luck until the next day. Fast forward a couple of decades from that time and you witness a completely different phenomenon. First of all, I primarily go to the Internet to get my information. While college libraries still exist, they have computer terminals where rows of stacked books used to exist. In fact, if you have a computer at home, you can work until the wee hours of the morning… and most students are doing this now. Internet sales are a growing aspect of business for Barnes & Noble and Borders. Additionally, Amazon, which started with sales of books, has created a retailing behemoth with many products from Internet sales.

Another interesting occurrence is that more people get their news from the television, their computer, or handheld PDA. To the chagrin and disappointment of many, local newspapers are shrinking or closing down. The whole concept of buying 30 or more books to make up your set of encyclopedias is very different for many people. This information is now accessed through various internet sites.

Convergence

Chances are the technology we have will lead to increasing convergence. We are already seeing the distinction between televisions and computers blur. Using Hulu and Netflix, we can watch favorite television programs on our computers. And televisions are gaining increased processing power that allows them to act in ways similar to computers.

How does one explain the difference between computers and television in regard to YouTube? You can get parts of your old favorite television programs on YouTube, but also millions of homemade videos and other programming that television networks and television production companies had nothing to do with. People now have the ability to create their own television programming. More than 100,000 videos are posted to YouTube every month. CBS, NBC, ABC, and Fox are minor players now in terms of video production when compared to this output by amateurs.

Again, this is not happening just in the U.S. On a recent visit to South Africa, I went to a number of villages that, in 1968, were under apartheid and technically and economically disadvantaged. Now, these villages have computers and televisions and cell phones. In the slums of Brazil and India and many other countries, a growing number of poor people, who may still struggle to access clean water, know about computers.

The Internet has changed the whole spectrum of how communication takes place. People can access worlds they could never before, and it does not matter where they are. And the devices used, whether telephones that act as cameras and camcorders, or computers that function as televisions, have functionality that increasingly crosses over from one device to the other.

The Computer Invasion

When I graduated high school in 1968, I worked at IBM, where I learned to use a keypunch machine, which was as large as a refrigerator. The printer attached to it was the size of a big desk. Now, all the equipment that took up a room is available with a handheld device like a Blackberry or iPhone. This opens up new worlds of information to me and all of us. I have access to more information and more types of information than I ever imagined. Whether ordering fast food, or going to the amusement park, or getting money from the ATM, you are probably interacting more with computers than people to get what you need.

The changes we are experiencing are not just with information. Computers affect the toys we play with. As a kid, I would go to friends' homes and play with action figures. My sister and her friends played with dolls. Now kids play with video games and three dimensional chess or hangman on a small screen. The youngest members of our society interact with toys and each other in ways very different than kids of their age did 40 years ago. I had the daughters of a friend over at our beach house during the summer and they spend more time surfing the Internet than surfing the ocean. Their lack of interaction with each other and their constant interacting with the PC is amazing to watch. To be sure, it's a different type of interaction. They are very content with their PC for hours at a time. When you think about play, this is not only reserved for kids. Adults are almost as addicted to computers as youngsters. It's difficult to carry on a conversation with some people without them working on their PDA at the same time. Unfortunately, some people also try to drive their cars and use the PDA, simultaneously, more than is necessary. Computers once thought of as strictly for businesses, are now in millions

of homes. In fact, it is not uncommon for lights, air condition-
ers, music systems and kitchen devices to now be totally controlled by computers in the home. This may have seemed like
science fiction 40 years ago, but it is commonplace now.

New Vocabulary

There are a number of words that exist now that are new
and reflect on how dramatically things have changed. Here are
a few we all know, but never heard of a decade or so ago:
Google, blog, Twitter, Face book, YouTube, Linked-In, and
Yahoo. These are not just new businesses, but represent important and vital ways by which people communicate. Interestingly
enough, if we go back 20 years, we can add to this list the
Internet and e-mail. We connect to others in ways very different than people connected before. Instant information transfer
and communication is coming about on a global scale.

Tectonic Shifts Taking Place in our Society

There are tectonic population shifts occurring as we speak.
Tectonic usually refers to changes in the plates of the earth,
but here I am referring to tectonic shifts in our society. The
Hispanic population, which represents 50 percent of total
population growth in the U.S., is an example. Asians, African
Americans, and other minority groups are becoming a greater percentage of the population, and this change will cause
a change in our vocabulary. Consider that we now say that

minority groups will soon become a majority of the population. This is not grammatically correct, of course, and we will have to change the words that we eventually use to describe groups of diverse population units.

By the time today's kindergarteners reach middle age, by about 2050, their society will be completely different than ours. How we define ourselves, relate to others, what we learn, where we live, how we educate our children, will all change.

We can see these changes taking place in other countries. In 1968, Russia was part of a major empire called the USSR. What was the USSR now consists of numerous independent countries, with Russia being the largest. According to Goldman Sachs, future world economic growth will not come primarily from the U.S. or Western Europe or Japan, but from such countries as Brazil, Russia, India and China -- the so-called BRIC countries. It would not surprise me to see Africa become an engine of growth. The African continent is rich in raw materials and resources like gold, diamonds, manganese, and bauxite, just to name a few, as well as having a large population.

Such "developing" countries will determine how our world will function. The U.S. has for well over a century been known for its extraordinary wealth, yet we are now a debtor nation to China, which in 1968 was not as economically advanced. Our relations with the BRIC and other countries will be heavily influenced by our economic relationships with them.

Life is a Passing Train

Have you ever been on a train platform and waited for the train to come? The worst feeling is when the train doesn't stop but passes by and you are left hoping that the next train will come soon. Perhaps the train stops but it is too crowded and you wait, hoping that the next train will come soon so you can get on your way. You are left disappointed and angry that you were not able to board the train. You feel anxious because you are uncertain when the next train will come, or if you do know the timetable, whether there will be space enough for you to board. Life is like a passing train, and if you don't get on board, it will pass you by and you will never get to your destination.

When we talk about change, change is already taking place and we have to face up to it or be left behind. We will have to learn how to maneuver, both as individuals and as a society. There's the corollary of how, if you put a frog in hot water, it will jump out, but if you put it in warm water and gradually heat it, it will stay there until it is cooked. You can let change sneak up on you and cook you, or jump at it and stay afloat. You, I, and everyone else in our society will change. We have no choice. Our choices are in how we deal with change and how capable we are at using change to our advantage.

In the next chapter we will explore how we think differently about this whole process.

Thought Stimulators

Ask Yourself:

1. Is what I'm doing aligned with my purpose?

Think of what you are doing in a variety of ways: where you live, who you are with (significant other), how you are living, where you work. Answer: Yes, No, Not totally. Be specific and explain your answer.

Think of what you are doing, where you live, who you are with, where you work. This is a beginning point to think about your change process. Usually there are several areas where you might feel that what you are doing is aligned with what your overall purpose is, and other areas where that might not be the case. Where you are living may make you happy, but not who you are with. You might be happy with your job, but not the company you work for because it is not aligned with your values and how you see your future.

The best way to think about this question is to draw a circle as if you were the "sun "and then have other circles almost like "planets" that surround this sun. Put a plus on the "planets" where things are aligned with your purpose and minus where they are not. Those "planets" may be the job, certain family members or friends. The "planets" may be your house, car or work commute. Get as detailed and specific as you can. This is a beginning point. Of course, rare is the person whose every situation is perfectly aligned with their values and needs.

Plus, people are always in a state of flux and things change. However, you can make changes that bring how you live your life into closer alignment with your values and needs. Get creative and put "moons" around those "planets." Do you have more pluses than minuses? Is there any relationship you notice among the planets?

2. How satisfied am I with my present situation?

Think of your present situation in a variety of ways: your job, your personal life, your key relations, and your geographic location. Answer: Yes, Somewhat, No, Yes but... (Be specific and explain your answer).

Think about your present situation: job, key relationships, and geographic location. Elaborate as much as possible on what is going well in each of these situations and then what is not going well. For the most part you will probably not get a definite "yes" or "no" answer; instead you will get a "yes but," and that's where you want to elaborate. That's how you decide what to change in your life.

3. What three aspects of your life that have changed in the last 10 years?.

Be specific: jobs, personal relationships, financial situation, professional accomplishments, children, education, location, housing, et al.

Some are surprised to see what aspects of their life have changed and that the situation they are in is so different when compared to 10 years ago. If you have children, they may have moved out of the house. You may be now in graduate school or received a graduate degree. You may have moved from an apartment to a house or to a bigger house. Outlining these changes over the last 10 years will shed some light over what might be possible over the next 10 years.

4. What three aspects of your life do you think will be changing in the next 10 years? And why do you think they will change?

Be specific: jobs, personal relations, financial situation, professional accomplishments, children, education, location, housing, et al.

Now that you have outlined the types of things that have changed and how they have changed, now you can better forecast changes over the next 10 years. Be as specific as possible, given the circumstances you might be facing -- retirement, a promotion, your financial situation, and the economic/financial/housing circumstances of your spouse, children, and even your parents. How will these affect you over the next 10 years?

5. *How will you play the back half of your life? What do you think will change in the back half and what will be similar?*

In sports, you can usually perform very well or poorly the first half of the game but your performance in the second half will dictate whether you "win" or not. How will you change things in the future -- or will you continue to make the same plays in the future as in the past? Hopefully, you will want to do some things differently. If the back half is to be better, what do you need to change, and how will you make those modifications?

6. *What are three things you can do differently to improve the back half of your life?*

Now that you have some thoughts on what might change, it is important to think about what you might do differently. If you don't do things differently, you will get the same results in the second half as the first half. If you are in a significant relationship that is not working for you, you will need counseling to improve the relationship or get out of it altogether. If your neighborhood is not safe, you need to think what you have to do differently to get out of that neighborhood. You may join or start a group to help make the changes necessary to improve the neighborhood. Almost all of us have three things worth changing in our lives. Now is the time to start thinking about what needs to change. In later chapters I will discuss how to start making changes. Right now we just want to get a feel for the specific aspects of our life that are going well and try to pinpoint what might be areas of concern. Too often, people just feel that things are going well, but they don't have a way of indicating specifically what it is. Also, it is critical to indicate what is going well so that you are not totally disappointed. Bad feelings have a way of clouding the good things that are in place.

Chapter 2
Think Differently

Change your thoughts and you change your world.

Norman Vincent Peale

In the previous chapter, I talked about why you might want to change. But to actually change, to engage in the actual mechanics of change, you have to change how you think. As Norman Vincent Peale noted, "when you change your thoughts, you change the world."

I try to avoid "psychobabble" and technical terminology, but here is a concept I think is helpful to our discussion: cognitive dissonance. Leon Festinger was a social psychologist particularly well known for his ties to this concept, which he helped popularize in the book *When Prophecy Fails*, which he co-wrote with Henry Riecken and Stanley Schachter.

Stated simply, cognitive dissonance is the idea that individuals have motivational drives, but sometimes these are at odds with one another, and when they are, the person experiences a certain anxiety or feeling of conflict -- or, as Festinger called it, cognitive dissonance. An example is of a person who says he or she believes in living a healthy lifestyle but smokes or does not exercise. Either the person has to start exercising or stop smoking, or has to change his or her belief that a healthy lifestyle is worthwhile.

An acquaintance says she believes one's time is important and therefore it is important to be punctual, but is consistently late to appointments. This behavior sows the seeds of cognitive dissonance. Folks like her cannot have a set of beliefs inconsistent with their behavior without there being some internal conflict. Something has to give.

Let me give you another example more germane to our discussion. I'm referring to those who go through life saying they want to improve their situation, want to do this or accomplish that, but do nothing. You are reading this because you want to make changes. If you have the desire to change, if you say to yourself you want to change, but do not change, you too will experience cognitive dissonance. There is a dissonance between what you say and want, and what you are currently doing.

Most of us can go through life with this cognitive dissonance and we take it as a given that these contradictory lines of thought and behavior should compatibly exist. The natural tendency is to avoid dealing with our situation or procrastinate.

The role of procrastination

When we procrastinate, it is because we want to postpone dealing with issues. It is amazing how long we can go through life not trying to resolve the difference between what we believe and what we are doing that is against those beliefs. Why? Because we will do anything to avoid pain and discomfort, and change seems more painful than keeping the status quo.

We finally make changes when our yearning for something better outweighs the pain of dealing with the present. When we face our present situation head-on, we begin to see that our present behavior is not getting us what we want. In order to resolve a dissonance, we have to realize first that it exists. We have to think differently about how we will get our needs met and achieve success. Is there sometimes pain associated with looking yourself in the eye and facing your reality? You bet there is. But it outweighs just waiting for things to change. You know what happens when you ignore a toothache. It just grows into a bigger problem later, but it does not ever go away.

A friend I grew up with named Ricky didn't always attend classes when we were in school so he could socialize with some of our other friends. In fact, he was very popular at the time and always chided me for not cutting classes with him. He put off his studies and eventually dropped out of school because he couldn't keep up. Several years later, he talked about completing his high school diploma, but said he could not find the time. I saw Ricky recently when he was between odd jobs doing handyman work. He could not get anything permanent because he didn't even meet the minimum requirements for a high school diploma. He told me that he wished he had paid attention before and gone to class, because his present situation is very depressing for him.

Change your life by changing your relationships

A friend, George Fraser, has a great saying: You can change your life by changing your relationships. In fact, if Ricky had found other acquaintances to associate with when we were in school, maybe he would be in a different place today. These acquaintances may have kept him focused on finishing school.

Making the change, though, can be very difficult. Sometimes the difficulty comes from sources you may not recognize. This happened to an acquaintance I'll call Judith. For years, she said she wanted to lose weight. But every workday, she went down to the company cafeteria with two of her friends from her department, and all three consumed large quantities of food. There lunch was essentially comparable to a dinner! She always ate with the same two women. No surprise, Judith never lost weight.

But things changed for Judith when, within a short period, both two friends left the company to work elsewhere and Judith was forced to do something different. Another person in her department would, during lunch, go to the gym beforehand and eat afterwards. Judith liked this woman and wanted to get closer to her, so she started going to the gym rather than the cafeteria. To her surprise, she found she did not have much need for a big lunch, or even any lunch. It did not take long for her to start shedding the weight she had long said she wanted to lose. I hadn't seen her in about five or six months, when I encountered her and was amazed. She not only lost 30 pounds, she dressed differently, had a new hairdo and had a certain spring in her step.

Judith had changed, but she changed because she changed her relationships. After years of trying to change, circumstances forced her to change, and she took advantage of this opportunity. The people you associate with can greatly influence you -- how you live your life and how to well you reach your goals. If you associate with winners, you have a much better chance of becoming a winner than if you associate with underachievers.

One way to change yourself is to change the environment in which you live, and that importantly includes the people in your life. Our peer group has a lot of influence over our actions and behaviors. What we think is right or wrong, correct or incorrect, is largely determined by those we associate with on a frequent basis. There is a strong drive in all of us to be accepted by "the group." Whether that group is our family, club, department, sports buddies, or sewing group, part of belonging to the group is having a similar thought process. To think differently or raise thoughts contrary to the group can be a problem for some individuals. Although in some societies these communal values serve a very positive, reinforcing role, this dynamic can be an issue if taken to the extreme; group-think can have its problems if not put in the right perspective.

Beware of groupthink

Albert Einstein once noted that if we are in a group where everyone thinks alike, no one thinks very much. Groupthink happens in many ways. Consider the tale of the Abilene Paradox.

The Abilene Paradox was introduced by Jerry B. Harvey in his article, "The Abilene Paradox and other Meditations on Management." The name of the phenomenon comes from an anecdote in the article that Harvey uses to elucidate the paradox:

On a hot afternoon in Coleman, Texas, a family is playing dominoes on a porch, until the father-in-law suggests they take a trip to Abilene (53 miles north) for dinner. The wife says, "Sounds like a great idea." The husband, despite having reservations because the drive is long and hot, thinks that his preferences must be out-of-step with the group and says, "Sounds good to me. I just hope your mother wants to go." The mother-in-law then says, "Of course I want to go. I haven't been to Abilene in a long time."

The drive is hot, dusty, and long. When they arrive at the cafeteria, the food is as bad as the drive. They arrive back home four hours later, exhausted.

One of them dishonestly says, "It was a great trip, wasn't

it?" The mother-in-law says that, actually, she would rather have stayed home, but went along since the other three were so enthusiastic. The husband says, "I wasn't delighted to be doing what we were doing. I only went to satisfy the rest of you." The wife says, "I just went along to keep you happy. I would have had to be crazy to want to go out in the heat like that." The father-in-law then says that he only suggested it because he thought the others might be bored.

Everyone was unhappy, and when they thought about why they went to Abilene, they realized none of them wanted to go. They all agreed to make the trip because they thought the others wanted to go. This is groupthink.

We see this in situations involving management, friends, and family. When you consider the earlier examples of Ricky and Judith, you see groupthink coming into play. Ricky and his cohorts would all skip classes and hang out. They reinforced each other's decision that this was acceptable behavior. The same with Judith who would go to the cafeteria with her friends, sit in the same place and at the same time, and feel comfortable that they were all doing the right thing.

Groupthink, in fact, is fairly common in the business world. We see it a lot with product introductions. Senior management might have a goal to increase market share. The marketing and product development people then launch products that they are doubtful about but they need additional products to attract market share. The products are not successful, but the pressure to meet senior management demands was too strong to resist by delaying. Fear keeps anyone from saying that these poor products will not have their intended impact. Groupthink emerges as everyone goes along with decisions that they actually feel are suboptimal!

These are illustrations of what so often happens: People take the path of least resistance. In the Abilene situation, all the participants wanted to appease each other, thinking that the group's actions were what each of the other members really wanted to do. Only afterward did they realize that no one in the group wanted to go to Abilene.

The nature of most people is not to rock the boat (to use a cliché), not to cause conflict. Their fear is that their opinions and thoughts will not be accepted or given credence. People in groups tend to go along with the group's behavior. How many times have you been with a group of friends and go along with what the group wants to do because you think everyone else wants to do such-and-such, and you don't want to breed conflict?

Open the lens of your mind

Have you ever taken a picture with a camera and, because of a lack of light, wanted to take another picture? So you open the aperture of the lens to bring in more light, which provides more clarity for your second photo. Well our mind is similar.

I suggest you open the "lens" of your mind to get more focus. Go deeper into your thoughts and feelings and needs, and challenge yourself by looking at things from a different point of view. There is an American Indian proverb that goes something like, "Please grant that I don't criticize anyone until I have walked in their moccasins." Put yourself in other people's shoes. Don't be different for the sake of being different, but try to see things in a framework more broad and encompassing than how you typically view situations.

When creating a new product, creating a new service, or changing a product label, think more broadly than you typically do. For example, Dell Computer was quite an innovator when it began. It pioneered selling personalized computers, customized to each customer's desires, directly to customers. This enabled Dell to sell at a price lower than storefront retailers and made it a major player in the computer industry. Richard Branson has been a pioneer in business by always thinking differently. From Virgin Atlantic to Virgin America to Virgin Records, he is always coming up with new entrepreneurial business ideas. Innovations are born from thinking differently in business, and this applies to individuals as well. We will address this further when we talk later about rebranding.

Using the "right" frame of mind

I am sure you have heard about right-brained and left-brained thinking. Right-brained thinking is more intuitive, visual, big picture oriented, while left-brained thinking is more logical, detail oriented, and sequential. But in truth, we all need to use both sides of our brains. One side is not better than the other. We need to look at problems holistically, more broadly. And when we do use both sides of our brains, we are likely to devise better solutions and responses to our needs.

As we expand our mental capacity to view issues differently, we expand our ability to make decisions. If you find that your dominant ways of making decisions is logical, then make an effort to consider how you would interject feelings or values into your decision-making matrix. Some people mistakenly believe that innovation and creativity come only from right-brained thinkers. In truth, the holistic thinking process considers both right- and left-brain thinking.

Albert Einstein is a great example of someone who used both sides of his brain to arrive at his theories of the universe. Einstein did a lot of thinking about religion and science, and in many of his writings and presentations, it's almost like one side of his brain talked to the other. The right side talked about aspects of religion and how important it is and how it rules our lives and the left side talked about science and how it rules our lives. In 1941, at a symposium on science, philosophy, and religion and their relationships to the democratic way of life, he said even though science and religion are clearly separate from each other, nevertheless there exists between them strong reciprocal relations and dependencies.

We should emulate Einstein and not have one side of our brain -- or one way of thought -- be dominant. Instead, we need a strong symbiotic relation between both ways of thought. This applies to life in general. Example: The iPod was as much a creative product as a technological wonder.

Whether you know if your dominant form of thinking is right- or left-brained is not critical. What is critical is to know you have a greater repertoire of ability than you may presently be using, and you will benefit by tapping into those deep resources to think differently than you are presently doing.

As a society, we tend to think that success comes to those who are the smartest, who have the highest intelligence. We are led to believe that if we were just more intelligent, that would make a difference. Furthermore, intelligence is often equated with education level. Educational attainment is not always all it is cracked up to be. Some of the most successful CEOs have limited education experience. Richard Branson of Virgin, Michael Dell of Dell Computer, and Bill Gates of Microsoft all dropped out of either high school or college.

In *Emotional Intelligence,* Daniel Goleman argues that emotional maturity is a more important factor for determining future success than IQ. IQ is probably responsible for 4 to 10 percent of our success, with the remainder being dependent on such things as how we relate to others, work on a team, and use empathy and feelings when making decisions. Goleman called these non-IQ factors emotional intelligence.

Individuals who are at the top of their organizations or professions tend to have strong emotional intelligence. They relate well with people, understand what motivates people, and understand how organizations and people work together more effectively. They are the leaders of an organization. If you are to succeed in the ways you would like, you will need to develop your emotional intelligence. Don't use IQ as an excuse for why you do not succeed. You have a wide range of capabilities at your disposal to further your dreams.

Thinking globally and acting locally

"Thinking globally and acting locally" is a phrase you may have already heard. In the global economy, this refers not just to new markets one can access around the world, but to increased international communications, and the sharing of culture, foods, and customs across national boundaries.

In the past 30 years, one could see this happening in the restaurant industry. Three decades ago, Mexican restaurants were quite rare in much of the country, especially in those states away from the border shared by the U.S. and Mexico. Vietnamese, Thai, various Chinese (except for Cantonese) and other Asian restaurants were also few in numbers.

Today, you can find a wide selection of restaurants in Manhattan. And I'm talking about Manhattan, Kansas, not New York. Hunan Chinese, Cajun, Mexican, and Thai are just a few of the ethnic restaurants to be found in this Kansas college town. This phenomenon brings a global flavor to one's local surroundings, and you will find this not just across the U.S., but throughout much of the industrialized world.

Do not be complacent from your own ethnocentric standpoint, but view things from the perspective of others. It helps to have a wider appreciation and respect for others, as you can then work more effectively and behave in a different way. When thinking cross culturally, try to behave in ways similar to people in other cultures.

In fact, in a general sense, the world is divided into two types of cultures -- low context and high context. The characteristics of a low context culture include very explicit verbal messages, direct and clear communication, and a high focus on being very literal. I distinguish this from high context cultures, where the meaning of a message is derived from the context of the message and the role of the person communicating. In a high context culture, communication is rather indirect, not literal but subtle. The listener has to "read between the lines" and pay attention to non-verbal cues.

The United States and Europe are low context cultures, while Asia, Latin America, and Africa are generally high context cultures. When people from these two cultures interact, the effect can be jarring, as often happens when an American communicates with, say, Japanese. In Japanese culture, the meaning and the cues are largely nonverbal. Silence says a whole lot more than do those who speak quite a bit. When Americans want to come to an agreement, they give themselves two or three days. When there's a dinner, they get right down to business. High context cultures might take weeks to negotiate an agreement because the relationship is important. A meal is a time to get to know someone rather than get down to business. Americans who are more culturally sensitive regarding how they communicate, socialize, and use their time, will be more successful in Asia.

I have visited Turkey numerous times and wanted to do business with Turkish companies coming to the U.S., so I joined the Turkish Chamber of Commerce. I went to its managing director to talk about my doing team building and consulting with Turkish companies coming to the U.S. He asked to see one of my training sessions, which I let him do. Then he wanted another meeting to learn more about me. The entire process took time, but at the end, he was comfortable with me and was most helpful.

In another situation, I was involved with the negotiations related to an American company that wanted to purchase a Turkish company. The negotiations took place over two years. Each meeting would result in our setting up another meeting. At each meeting, the patriarch of the family who owned the company we wanted to acquire was always in the room, but did not say anything to us. We assumed he did not speak English.

The patriarch's Western-educated son would look to the patriarch at the end of each meeting (who was virtually always rolling his prayer beads), and then would say to us that we had a very good meeting, and then would arrange another meeting. One time he asked us to take a trip down the Bosporus, a major river, to see some of the wonderful sights of Turkey. We knew it was important to show we liked them and their country, so we went. By working at their pace, we demonstrated we had patience, and by taking trips, such as the one on the

Bosporus, we demonstrated we were appreciative of the great history of their country.

At the end of one meeting, I asked the interpreter where I could get prayer beads like those of the patriarch. I was told to go to a certain store near the famous Blue Mosque. At our next meeting, I pulled the prayer beads out, and showed them to the patriarch. He said -- much to my surprise, in English -- that they were very good beads, and then asked where I got them. The point was to show him that I was interested in his culture.

It should not have surprised us he knew English since so many people in Turkey and other countries speak our language. Then he said, "I think we are making very good progress and at our next meeting, we can sign a deal." I can't say my buying the beads was important to our finalizing the deal, but I showed there was something more important to me than corporate financial gain.

The son subsequently told me: "We wanted to know if you would treat our employees like family, which is how we treat them. We didn't want to turn them over to just anyone." Money wasn't the most important factor. This was working from a low context situation to a high context one.

How people need to free their minds

To *be better than you believe*, you need to free your mind from the tasks at hand. Unfortunately we live in a world of what we "ought to" do and "should" do. We are stuck in a lot of routine. We become a slave to history rather than finding a new way to look at things.

In *Brave New World,* Aldus Huxley talked about a society where to be happy, people needed to just give in and let others handle things for them. It was a place where people did not have to make certain choices. Huxley was writing a satire of a totalitarian society.

But we are often totalitarian in our minds because we do things in a prescribed way rather than in new ways. That's why it is important not to be a slave to the past. When we think of the future, we need to consider what the future *could* be like -- not what it *ought* to be. Once we start thinking like this, we can begin thinking differently.

The full aspect of having a future orientation or breaking from the past has to do with how we let go and redefine how we act. We need to say goodbye to how we have always acted, and kick the habit of looking at things only from the perspective of how we have always looked at things. Only then can we redefine our relationships with our families, friends, employer, colleagues, and others. Looking at things differently is critical when starting down the road to thinking differently. Our situations initially will not change, but how we look at situations will change, and that begins the process of changing ourselves.

There is an old story of the child and the three stonecutters which helps to illustrate this. A child saw three stonecutters on the road and asked the first, "What are you doing?" "I'm trying to carve a rock," he said. Then the child asked the second the same question, and he replied, "I'm in the process of building a wall." When the child asked the third the same question, he said, "I'm in the process of building a cathedral." They had the same tools and rocks, but very different views of what they were doing.

Sometimes the view you have of what you are doing depends on the context in which you operate. The same behavior can generate a narrow view or a much broader view, and the view you take can change the meaning of that behavior to you, and the significance of that behavior in your life. The man who viewed his work as carving a rock had a much more limited view of his effect on society than the man who viewed his work as part of the building of a cathedral.

Martin Luther King, in a speech to sanitation workers he gave shortly before he was assassinated, said that if you are going to be a street cleaner, be the best street cleaner in the world and take pride in your work. Such work was no less noble than the work of others, even if others got paid more money.

Another situation that illustrates the point relates to Marty Markowitz, borough president of Brooklyn, N.Y. To non-New Yorkers, New York City is Manhattan. The so-called "outer boroughs" -- Brooklyn, Queens, the Bronx, and Staten Island -- are viewed as less critical. Even some of those who live in New York view the outer boroughs as somehow of a lesser status, witness the fact that they are called the "outer boroughs."

Not Marty Markowitz. Each borough has its own elected president and Markowitz, as Brooklyn's borough president, may be the borough's greatest advocate. A bit factiously, he calls Manhattan the "Brooklyn of the North." He takes great pride in Brooklyn, and never misses an opportunity to promote his home borough. This may sound like meaningless political posturing, but in fact, Markowitz's advocacy on behalf of his borough has had a real effect on Brooklyn in the form of economic development. Money has poured into Brooklyn because of Markowitz's grandstanding. How you view situations matters. I was born and raised in Brooklyn and will always feel a part of that place regardless of how many other places I live.

Be like the little engine that could

When I think of the cheerleading of Marty Markowitz, I think of the story "The Little Engine That Could." The engine said, "I think I can, I think I can," as it went up the hill. No matter what position you might be in, the story illustrates how you can accomplish great things. How, if you are optimistic and work hard, you can *be better than you believe*.

In Cape May, N.J., some hotels in recent years have suffered from declining business, while others have prospered. One large hotel complex there has been in operation for many years and has hosted presidents and other notable figures. For its guests, each day this hotel sets up rows of chairs and yellow umbrellas on the beach directly across the street from the hotel. Waiters from the hotel bring guests food and drinks.

It is a public beach, but only this hotel had its chairs and umbrellas and wait staff on the beach. Other hotels felt they could not compete on the beach. That is, until a nearby motel decided it would take on this behemoth. This motel had been a budget facility -- nice, clean, and serviceable, but definitely not for high priced luxury clientele. It decided to rebrand itself. They realized that by investing in services that the public considers a priority they could attract a wider range of clients. It remodeled its façade and, on the beach directly across the street, it started planting bright pink umbrellas. It worked. This motel is now quite popular and I notice just about every time I pass by, its sign says, "No vacancy." It was the little engine that could.

There are plenty of other examples. I worked at Colgate-Palmolive, a consumer products company, which was much smaller than its major competitors, which include Procter & Gamble and Lever Brothers. But when you go into stores, you will find its products, which include Colgate toothpaste, Irish Spring soap, and Palmolive dishwashing detergent, positioned well on the shelves against the products of its global competitors. Colgate-Palmolive shareholders do pretty well when compared to those of its larger competitors, as measured by shareholder value, P/E ratio and the like. Bigger is not necessarily better. This is a company that constantly says, "I think I can, I think I can," and it does what it thinks it can do. If you are to *be better than you believe*, you need the courage to think of yourself differently than you have been. You need to believe you really can achieve what you want to achieve.

Sow the seeds of innovation

When you begin to act like the little engine that could, that is when you begin to sow the seeds of innovation. Think of innovation: Where do creative thoughts come from? If you go back to the 1500s, you will find Gutenberg as he decided he wanted to devise an entirely different way of producing books. That goal led him to invent movable type. Before that, books were handwritten one at a time. Gutenberg had to think differently from other people to create his moveable type.

Let me give you a more recent example. Years ago I worked for IBM and Digital Equipment Corp. Apple Inc., maker of Apple computers, iPods and iPhones, was not on the radar screen of either of these corporations, which were huge at the time. Today, DEC is out of business and IBM has had to reinvent itself. When I recently looked, Apple's market cap was significantly larger than IBM's. Apple was a nobody, but is now a behemoth. It got to this position by breaking free from its past and redefining its markets. The recorded music industry has changed forever because of the iPod, and the smart phone industry has been transformed, thanks to the iPhone. And the iPad is taking tablet computing mainstream.

Before Tim McCann, those who wanted to buy flowers would order from a store. After McCann started 1-800-Flowers, people could call a central number and, using a credit card, have flowers delivered virtually anywhere in the country. McCann, like Apple's Steve Jobs and Gutenberg, was a true visionary. It is also interesting to note that McCann started his career as a social worker in a residential treatment facility. He sees his business as part of his caring attitude toward people, which helped him devise his business model for 1-800-Flowers.

Many of us know of the non-profit used clothing store chain called Goodwill, and view them as places for cheap second hand goods, and they used to be right. But Goodwill has been thinking differently about itself, and has begun to get higher quality, second hand clothing from well-known retailers. It has changed its merchandising strategy, and is now a viable destination for those who want to freshen up their house or closet with fairly trendy goods. As part of this upgrade, the store façades have been improved, with bright blue-and-white signage that is more inviting and attractive.

Another visionary, as I mentioned earlier, is Sir Richard Branson of Virgin Atlantic, a U.K.-based airline. He has a simple philosophy: "Screw it, just do it." Calculate the risks, chase your dreams, be bold and have fun. He started out small but successfully challenged some of the world's largest airlines, including the U.K.'s own, British Airlines. Virgin Atlantic competed with great service and amenities.

Thinking differently is something that, ultimately, you need to do. Only then can you make the changes you want -- and can achieve. It's useful, in going through this process, to assess how your values can help or hinder you in your process of change. We will explore this in the next chapter.

Thought Stimulators

Ask yourself:

1. What three things bring the most joy into my life?

Many times when we think about what we're doing, we realize we don't always get as much satisfaction as we might. We settle for the status quo: The money we're making is fine, but it's not bringing us any joy; the relationship is fine, but it is not bringing us any joy. When you experience joy, then you are really experiencing excitement in your life. Joy is beyond just "fine."

2. What are the three biggest concerns in my present situation?

Your present situation refers to your personal relationships, financial situation, job, lifestyle, etc. Take a look at all the different aspects of your life, and then talk about your concerns -- about where you are living, your job, your significant other, your educational situation, your financial situation, your spiritual journey.

3. What area of my life needs to change to bring me more fulfillment? Why do I want to make this change?

This is the point where you really begin talking about moving from a status quo situation to one that will bring you a lot more fulfillment and satisfaction. Unfortunately, many of us just settle for the situation we are in because we don't think we deserve a change or can make a change. Think about areas that will bring you fulfillment instead of being in the status quo and just being satisfied. Answer that question by digging deep into your concerns and feelings.

4. Write a statement in the future tense that is in the affirmative, which describes the area of your life that needs to change. Write it as if it were solved.

For example, if you are unemployed, the affirmative is: Now I have a good job. If you are in a poor relationship, you might write: We have worked out our differences and now have a good relationship. Or, I have ended my poor relationship and am now in a very positive one.

5. Identify three things you need to do to bring this change about. Be specific.

At this point, you want to identify and clarify three things you want to change -- be as specific as possible about what you want to do differently.

6. Describe what you think are the three biggest challenges you face that will keep you from reaching your goals.

An example of an individual who faced incredible

challenges was Melody Gardot. Melody was studying fashion and design at a Philadelphia community college when she was riding her bike and was hit by a car. She suffered massive trauma to her brain, spine, and legs. She was unable to walk or talk for a long time, and she had significant memory loss. At a young age she had a tremendous challenge that threatened her life and future profession. She did play guitar and piano in school. Through months of music therapy, she was able to re-channel the nerves in her brain to fully develop her musical capability. Today, Melody is a widely publicized jazz artist and her last album went platinum in Europe. Think of the challenges you face and how, by thinking differently, you can achieve your goals.

Chapter 3
Anchoring Your Values

The key to the ability to change is a changeless sense of
who you are, what you are about and what you value.

Stephen Covey

"Values." This word is frequently seen in today's media: personal values, moral values, family values, religious values, ethical values, democratic values. Its widespread use is enough to confuse anyone. This chapter is about values, and rather than just talk vaguely about them, I have chosen to use a model of 11 values that comes from the work of L. Robert Kohls and F.R. Klockhohn. This model provides a framework for understanding values and ways to anchor them.

What are values? They are very important, enduring beliefs and ideas about what is desirable. At their most basic, they influence our behaviors and serve as guidelines that regulate our actions. Think of values as your life's compass. The purpose of a compass is to point you in the direction you want go.

Likewise with values; they help you navigate through the seas of life. Values are instruments that help determine where you want to go, which direction you want to go in to achieve your goals, and what tools you want to use to accomplish your life's ambitions.

The literature relating to values contains endless different values, far more than one can usefully employ in life. That is why the 11 identified by Kohls and Klockhohn are so useful. Note, these are really not 11 values per se, but 11 spectrums of values, which is why I refer to them as "value spectrums." I describe two values, each at the opposite ends of the particular spectrum, and between them are gradations. Most people are not at the extremes, but somewhere between.

Value Spectrum 1: Personal control versus fate

Personal control is a value indicating that one wants and expects a fair degree of control over one's life and environment. This contrasts with fate, with which one believes external influences greatly control our lives, over which we have little or no control.

Members of various religions take the view that the teachings of the religion and the "will of God" dictate what happens to them. In other communities, skills and abilities are believed to determine one's outcomes and drive one's fate, and the outcome is based on the individual's personal will.

Most people, of course, fall somewhere in between,

thinking they have some control over their lives, but that fate also plays a role. I worked on a project team in Egypt that included several Egyptian product managers and engineers; the team laid out the critical path for a new product launch. We took into account all of the variables we could think of for a successful launch within an eight month period, which would enable us to capture market share from our competitors.

After the two-day meeting, where we had everyone agreeing to the plan, I asked the director of the group whether he believed we would be able to fully execute our goals as indicated. He said with a strong degree of confidence, "There is no doubt in my mind we will make this happen... Inshallah!" Well, that was a very important statement. You see, Inshallah means in Arabic, If God or Allah wills it. In other words, despite the best laid out plans from very knowledgeable and Western educated professionals, the feeling still exists that none of this will happen unless God or Allah wills it. To be sure, they feel they can impact the business, but there is still this other factor which plays a role in their beliefs and their behavior.

Value Spectrum 2: The individual versus the group or community

Those who believe the individual is prominent, also value privacy and believe that every individual is unique and special. The individual is their main focal point.

Those who believe the group is more prominent have a

different set of values. Privacy, for example, may be taken as an indication one is exclusionary of others. For such people, the group is their main focal point, and the group is the major organizing factor of the community.

Also, individualists value self-reliance, while group-oriented folks find it desirable to be dependent on the group for their needs and wants. In such groups, individuals have a much stronger need to identify with others rather than their own individuality.

The United States is a country where individualism and self-reliance is given considerable value. Many Latin American, African, and Asian countries stress community, where the desires and wishes of the family override the individual. For example, in community-oriented cultures, the decision to marry is not made solely by the man and woman involved, but requires the bride and groom's parents to agree and even their entire extended families. This is even the case in some communities in America and Europe, but the degree of involvement in the life-changing decisions vary according to a number of factors, most importantly the values of the key players.

There is an African saying that has been mainstreamed recently by Hillary Clinton using it as the title of a book she wrote: "It takes a village to raise a child." This concept speaks to the fact that rearing children and giving youth feedback on their behavior is not just the responsibility of the parents. The community plays a pivotal role. Child rearing is a responsibility that extends beyond the parents to the entire community.

All members of the community have a stake in the outcome, which accounts for their involvement with all the community's children.

Value Spectrum 3: Orientation toward time

Some are more future oriented than others. They value planning and goal setting, and focus on what is to come and how they might influence it. Others focus on the past; tradition and history are much stronger guidelines for their behavior and how they approach their current situations.

We all have probably met people who exhibit these different time value orientations. There's the person who is the big thinker, the visionary, who looks to the future. Others are future oriented in that they set goals and create plans to achieve these goals.

At the other end of the spectrum are those fairly sedentary in their thinking, who tend to do things as they have always done. They move through their personal and professional lives essentially repeating themselves, giving little thought to what the future might bring and how they might make their future better. Others are very present oriented, living "one day at a time." They look more to the present, rather than the future or the past.

The other issue about time is that some people feel they have plenty of time to do things or start on certain projects. This orientation may cause them to procrastinate or put off doing things until the last minute. When I was in college, I could not help but notice how students handled their term papers. Some would start very early so they could pace themselves. Others would wait to the last minute and cram it all in, not even sleeping until everything was complete.

Value Spectrum 4: Direct versus indirect communicators

Direct communicators are candid, to the point, and specific in their communication. Indirect folks are subtler. They imply rather than clearly articulate. Often, what is between the lines is more important than what is on the lines -- what is unsaid is more revealing than what is said. An indirect person values both verbal and nonverbal communication, while the direct person values more what is said and what is done.

Witness for example the tale of Chauncey Gardiner, played by Peter Sellers in the film, "Being There," which is based on a book of the same title by Jerzy Kosinski. This is an entertaining movie that portrays Chauncey, a gardener, making simple statements which everyone feels are allegories about what will happen with the economy. For instance, when he states that when you plant in the right season you will see the bloom in due time, people feel he is talking about the economy improving soon. He was using gardening as a metaphor for the economy. It is a wonderful farce and shows how people can read between the lines and assume all types of things.

Certainly life imitates art in many ways -- consider Alan

Greenspan, former chairman of the Federal Reserve, known for making public statements regarding the US economy. The meanings of his pronouncements were not always readily apparent. He was an indirect communicator. Ronald Reagan, whom the media bestowed with the sobriquet, The Great Communicator, was known for making simple, direct and easily understood public pronouncements.

Value Spectrum 5: Equality versus hierarchy

Those who believe in equality have a value system in which all people are created equal, we should treat everyone the same, and individuals have considerable freedom to determine the roles they will play in life. Those who have a hierarchical value system believe that rank and status are highly important, people have their place in society, and the rights one has depends on one's age, sex, or even position in a group. With such believers, it is difficult to break out of the roles they ascribe to individuals. This is more apparent in older European societies where kings and queens ruled.

The "old boys network" was a hierarchical value system, in which those whose families were part of the network, and those who went to certain prestigious schools, were placed high on the food chain. At the same time, those who came from poorer backgrounds and went to less elite schools were relegated to lower status jobs and lower status spouses. More egalitarian communities -- Silicon Valley seems like one -- take a more equality-oriented view. Someone with brains, creative ideas, ambition, and ability can make it in such communities whatever their background, whereas in more hierarchical communities, they may be shunned.

Value Spectrum 6: Being versus doing

For those who value being, thinking is important and contemplation is valuable. Their view of themselves: I define myself based on who I am rather than based on my external accomplishments. They do not focus on the material, but more on the spiritual, the reflective.

For those who value the doing, what they do defines who they are. For them, hard work is highly valued because it boosts their self-esteem. They define themselves by external factors and all the things they have accomplished in their lives. An extreme form of the "being" value is the life led by those in certain religious communities under vows of chastity such as monks and nuns. Those who work on Wall Street, where value is measured by the size of one's income, might be considered an extreme form of the "doing" value.

Value Spectrum 7: Harmony versus competition

Those who believe in competition believe it is the most effective means to bring out the best in people. Survival of the fittest is best because by competing, they think they can get the best work done and bring out the best in society.

Those who value harmony believe we are all in this world together and competition undermines the group. If too competitive, the individual can hurt the community. The community is better off when individuals strive for more balance in their lives and in their social and professional circles, versus the competitive individuals who pit themselves against others and like to be in social and professional settings where competition reigns.

A good example of a very competitive profession is sales, where salespeople earn based on commission. They are constantly striving to make their goals. Their promotion and salary is highly dependent on whether they meet certain quotas. Musicians, on the other hand, who work in an orchestra, will strive to be more harmonious with other musicians during a performance. Musicians realize that the success of their work is dependent upon how well their fellow musicians play.

Value Spectrum 8: Spiritual versus material

Materially oriented individuals believe the best way to success is to acquire more objects. They want to generate wealth, and the more objects and wealth they have, the more successful they are.

Believers in spirituality view introspection and spiritual growth as one's primary goals, and that to grow spiritually is more important than to acquire more possessions. For these individuals, success is measured by spirituality. Many followers of New Age beliefs are oriented to following their soul, while those in the business world tend to generally focus on materiality. Does this mean no business professionals are spiritual? Not at all. But certainly the primary driver in business is to increase material wealth.

Value Spectrum 9: Formality versus informality

Those who believe in formality believe in tradition and ritual. Being formal is a sign of respect and importance. Informality is a belief in the value of being spontaneous. The casual is preferred over the formal. Examples of these two ends of the value spectrum are seen in many urban business centers where some wear suits to work and others more informal attire. Sure, some of this is a function of one's work and the requirements of one's employer, but even within an office is usually found a range of attire, depending on the values of the individuals.

More generally, visit New York and California, and you will find people in offices dressed more formally and even more fashionably in New York than those in California, who tend toward the informal. People's behavior can be formal versus informal: hand shakers versus huggers; those who do not smile when meeting a stranger and are all business versus those who frequently smile and engage in small conversation. All of these reflect a person's values.

Value Spectrum 10: Change versus stability

Some value stability and believe in tradition, heritage, and keeping situations stable. In fact, they may feel that changing, fluid situations are undesirable. Others view change as positive and representing growth. For them, change is the natural way to proceed in life

My son and his millennial friends who worked with him in investment banking would never wait around 20 years for a gold watch at retirement. They expect to change jobs every few years to avoid boredom. On the other hand, there are some people who are baby boomers, who have no problem with the stability provided by working for one employer for many years.

Experts say most people will work for over seven companies in their lifetime. This has changed from 50 years ago when the average was closer to four companies in a lifetime. Of course, this may differ depending on one's profession, geographic location and education, but values are the underlying determinant.

Value Spectrum 11: Self help versus birthright

Those who believe in their birthright believe their lineage, heritage, and family background are essential to their success and feel entitled to the benefits of their birthright. Those who believe in self-help believe initiative and work get you where you need to go, and individual accomplishments are essential

BEING BETTER THAN YOU BELIEVE

qualities for success in life.

Birthright is valued in class-oriented societies, such as those once found in Britain and India. The U.S., while certainly not entirely classless, has been less class oriented than many other societies, which is a major reason why the U.S. has more immigrants than any other country. Because other societies have birthright as the main value driver, people come to the U.S. in search of opportunities unavailable in their own country.

Right or Wrong?

Among these value spectrums, there is no right or wrong. Individuals can subscribe to the extremes, or any blend of values along the spectrums. Which values they chose determines what direction they will take in life and how they get their needs met.

For example, when you look at the behavior of individuals in certain situations, you find they choose certain values based on how they think society should be run. In many African and Asian countries, fate is important, but in the U.S., many feel they have more control. But we should not stereotype these values as being specific to certain cultures. In the U.S., though more an Anglo culture than any other type, we place much value in equality, whereas in England, which is of course the source of the Anglo culture, hierarchy is more valued than in the U.S. You can have a similar framework but still end up with different values.

Consider a European culture such as Germany's. The Germans generally believe in being much more direct than indirect. At the same time, they believe personal control and the rights of the individual are prominent and extremely important.

Some African cultures, on the other hand, exhibit more reliance on the family and community. Also valued are harmony and formality, along with birthright. An individual's birthright can determine the rights and benefits they get in the family. The age order of children may determine their rights and status in the family, rather than accomplishments. Of course, one can see this in other cultures, too. Who ascends to the throne in England is determined by placement in the birth order of the monarch's children.

Spirituality is also expressed in different ways. Western societies have many well-organized religions, while Asia's Buddhist culture is based on how you live. In the latter case one does not need an organized religion, and being religious is not the same as being spiritual. In fact, many people in the West are not religious from the standpoint of regularly attending a church, synagogue, mosque or other gathering place, but as individuals they try to incorporate their spiritual beliefs into their everyday life practices.

Often when you observe the conflicts people feel in organizations, it is because of a conflict of values they have. Often an individual will have a strong underlying feeling that the company they are working for is just not the right place for them, but they can't pin down the reasons. It may be that the company does not allow him or her to fully express their beliefs about helping others or caring for the environment.

Allen, a chemical engineer, worked a long time for an industrial chemicals contractor. He began to feel his employer was engaged in activities that threatened the sanctity of animal and plant life because it made products harmful to the environment. This went against Allen's values, prompting him to conclude he could no longer work at that type of company. It doesn't mean Allen was right or wrong, but had a value clash he recognized and did something about. He quit his job to work for a scientific institute where he develops new inventions geared to solar energy and environmental conservation. In this position Allen feels that he is does something much more worthwhile and beneficial.

Beatrice was once an English school teacher. Although at one point she was disillusioned with teaching in the public school system, she didn't want to just go work for any corporation. Her values were still very much aligned with furthering the education of others, but did not feel she was making the progress she expected because of what she termed bureaucratic issues. So she started working for a publishing company as an editor and has been happy ever since. She has a lot more independence and control over her work and is able to see the good results of her efforts. She is having a greater impact on children by providing books that she feels are more exciting and relevant to the needs of children today.

The same type of conflict came up for a sales executive named Roberto. His employer wanted to move him from the southwest part of the U.S. to the northeast. But family and community were more important to Roberto than a job, a promotion, and more money. His family and community were in the southwest, so he told his employer he would not move. Instead, he negotiated with the company to pursue his career where he is.

This career move worked well for him, and for the last 15 years he hasn't had to move but has still been promoted and enjoyed professional success. One cannot always negotiate like this, but he was able to pinpoint the values clash he faced and have his employer meet his needs while, at the same time, being able to meet the needs of the employer.

Conflict between work and family values

Many women value their careers but also want time to have children and be good mothers. Increasingly, organizations realize they need ways to resolve the value clash that occurs when women want a family and yet also pursue their careers. These women need to feel free to start a family and not have to leave the company in order to progress professionally, and many companies are trying to accommodate the needs of these women while also meeting the needs of the organization. Companies do not want to lose valuable human talent that has knowledge and skills valuable to the company.

Not only women are experiencing this conflict between family and work, it should be noted, but men too. Now more than ever I see men wanting to spend time with their family. More progressive companies have parental leave policies that allow men to leave to take care of children just like women. Inflexible organizations create serious value clashes when they refuse to provide men the same parental-leave rights as women.

Value conflicts occur at home as well as at work. George and Judy had different perspectives regarding spending money. They both worked and earned about the same amount of money as professionals. However, Judy was more frugal and believed in delaying gratification to meet the long term needs of the family. However, George felt that he was entitled to buy a new suit or watch whenever it suited him. A crisis occurred when Judy was using the family credit card to buy some food and the store indicated that their account was overdrawn. This situation caused Judy to confront George so they could talk more about how they were going to approach their spending patterns. George valued his relationship with Judy and didn't feel that his previous behavior was a problem. This caused them both to think about how they were going to budget their money and set up communication between them so they wouldn't have this situation happen again. While George still likes to purchase big ticket items, he is a lot more considerate of the family obligations than he was before. He found that by delaying certain purchases, he was able to demonstrate that he was more sensitive to Judy's concerns.

Another situation involved Juan and Alicia. Both of them were single and finally decided to get married. As a single man, Juan enjoyed a lot of freedom. He lived on his own. He didn't have to report to anyone about his comings and goings. He would spend his money and go on vacations whenever it suited him. Now that he was going to get married to Alicia, he realized that he needed to change if their relationship was going to be successful. He would have to collaborate with her regarding… well almost everything. This is not unlike the type of situation facing many couples about to get married. The key to success is communication, communication, communication. Alicia and Juan went to counseling ahead of time so they could learn how to be more respectful and receptive to the feelings of each other. This certainly helped to set up a strong foundation for the future. Juan ultimately found that his life was much more fulfilled because the strong communications between them have enabled him to talk about what is important to him and to incorporate her needs into his decision-making.

Paradigm shifting to change

In looking at the situation of trying to *be better than you believe*, and shifting your situation to improve it, getting really in touch with the values driving your behavior is vital. Many people don't take time to step back and understand the values that drive them, drive their families, and drive their careers. When you look at a situation where you have a gnawing feeling that something is not working, look at the values underlying your decisions and the situation. Often, this will reveal the key to understanding what is happening.

As individuals, we are extremely complex and have beliefs that underlie many of our values. These values are important as they influence how we behave and how we think, but these values are not always understood. When considering change, consider if your current beliefs work to get what you want. Do they work for or against you? If they work against you, change your beliefs.

For example, when I think of my own career, the choices I made and what has helped me and what has been getting in the way, I immediately see the role of values. At one point, I decided stability was important, so I would not move or relocate. But I was looking for a job and lived in Westchester County, the county directly north of New York City. Eventually, I realized that staying in the community would not work for me professionally. I changed my values and moved to Cincinnati, which opened up a new world for me.

To make the move, I had to challenge a basic belief I had, which was that by staying in the same place, I could get everything I wanted. I valued stability, but I decided stability did not have to be solely found where I lived. More important was having stability in my personal life. That was a value I never changed, and my wife and I have been married for over 30 years. The value of stability is still important, but I exercised it in a realm that worked for rather than against me.

Ultimately, that is the real test: Are your values getting you what you want? Do your values work for you or against you? Are your values facilitating your life's journey or causing problems? What other values could help you be successful? And what is success? Do you define it by what others say, or are there more fulfilling standards?

Many try to live the values of others as opposed to making their own choices. You need to question whether your values help you live the life you want, or are values decided by others, such as your parents, spouse, or employer.

It is not uncommon for kids to feel they have to live the life of their parents. One parent who tried to get her child to live her values was Audrey, who bought a vacation home in Florida. She bought the property, in part, because she believed her daughter would want the house when Audrey passed on. Yet in the 10 years since buying the house, the daughter has visited only once. Her daughter likes to vacation in different places, rather than going to the same place year after year, so returning time after time to a house in Florida was unappealing to her .

I asked Audrey's daughter why she hadn't been to Florida. Her response: the people were uninteresting and the nightlife limited. This is the type of value clash I often see across both families and organizations. The daughter understood her values, but Audrey did not fully appreciate and didn't express interest in her daughter's values. When I last spoke with Audrey, the issue was still not resolved. I don't think anything will change until Audrey dies, and then the daughter will sell the house. She has not yet told her mom, and probably never will. This is not uncommon. Not all value clashes can be amicably resolved.

How you live matters

A good friend, David, has a great greeting. When he meets someone, he asks: How are you living? David and his wife Marianne are from Maryland where he owned a candy store and she was an attorney. They had a big house in Maryland, with plenty of the trappings of status, including two Mercedes and several Rolex watches.

David thought he was happy, but at a certain point he began wondering if this was all life offered. Marianne felt similarly. When in their 50s, he sold the store, she retired from her federal government job, and they sold their big home in Maryland. The proceeds from the house and their savings went to buy a small house in Florida, and another in Spain, on the southern coast.

They were motivated by the desire to enjoy their money. The store and government job did not provide a desirable lifestyle. Those jobs provided plenty of material benefits, but the things they liked, such as sunshine and water activities, and being in a European culture, were available only in limited quantities.

Now in their 70s, they still visit their place in Spain, but spend the majority of their time in Florida. When you visit David, he is invariably wearing beachwear. He believes in following the sun, and owns no winter clothes.

He decided to live differently than he was, and Marianne agreed. Living by the standards of their friends and community wasn't really living, they figured, so they drastically changed their living situation. They are now happier and healthier than when in Maryland, and both feel they have more freedom and more control over their lives than before making these changes. They don't have the big house anymore but by their values, they are living very successful lives.

I know you are busy, but...

Sometimes it's all a matter of how you spend your time. We all make decisions regarding what we will spend our time on. Some of those decisions are conscious, and some are subconscious. Every day we face choices regarding how we will spend our time, who we will spend it with, and what we will be doing. How we spend our time will dictate, to a large degree, the progress we can make toward fulfilling our life goals. Time is a scarce resource. You can waste it, invest it, or spend it wisely.

Often when we say we are too busy to put attention to those areas that require change, it is a matter of the choices that we make, which is often guided by our values. Edith always said she wanted to go to the gym three days a week, but couldn't find the time because she was too busy. What the experts will tell you is that if you cannot find three days a week, then start with two and work your way up. The main thing is to set up a routine and then stick to it.

First she said that she would start at lunchtime, but that didn't work because it seemed like there were always meetings that overlapped with lunchtime. She didn't want to exercise at the beginning of the day because she would have to leave her house too early. Nor did she care to exercise at the end of the day, and get caught up in the rush hour. So she had a dilemma that required modifying her schedule and sacrificing time that seemed fixed in her mind.

Eventually, she was able to get a friend, whom she commuted with, to exercise with her at the beginning of the day. In fact, she set up a flex-time arrangement with her supervisor so she could come in two hours later than usual and make up the time at the end of the day. She was busy, but once she made up her mind that she valued her body more than the comfort of getting caught up in rush hour, she was able to make the necessary changes. We are all busy, but for the most part it's a matter of the choices we make regarding how we will spend our time.

When you begin to think how busy you are, take an inventory of how you spend your time and then ask yourself: Can I shave off a few hours a week toward a goal that I say I don't presently have time for? Allen was a police officer who decided he wanted to be a lawyer. He had a number of obligations that could easily get in the way of this goal. He had a wife, two children, and a mortgage. He was in his 30s and couldn't see any way to leave his full time job to go to school full time. He decided the best way to accomplish his goal was to go part time to law school. It would take four years instead of three, but once he was finished, it would be very beneficial.

This choice meant he had to severely curtail his social club activities, vacations, and even sleep. However, fast-forward to now, and Allen is a judge on a state supreme court. Was it worth it for him? You bet it was. How busy you are is always a matter of choices. What are you busy doing? Can you allocate your time differently in order to achieve a worthy goal? How you allocate your time is a matter of values.

It all comes down to how you visualize yourself, and that is what I want to talk about next.

Thought Stimulators

Ask yourself:

1. From the Living More Values list (see Appendix at the end of the book), identify the top 25 values that drive your life.

On this list are 377 values. Usually only a few really provide the compass for our life's direction and the choices we make. Identify the top 25.

2. From the list of your top 25 values, highlight the top four that are your key value drivers.

Explain why each of these is among your top four.

It is usually very difficult to go from 25 to four values. You might decide that courage is an important value that drives your life, but what drives courage is honor, bravery, and sacrifice and you want to include them as well. Think about the relationships of some values to others, and write down those most significant to you.

3. *Identify the top four values of your significant other.*

Are these aligned with your top four? Are there conflicts (be specific)?

This is a point where we really begin to see why some individuals get along and others don't. If you have a strong value of looking good, but your significant other believes in being practical and this is reflected in his or her dress and style of clothing, you and your spouse will be in conflict. If your spouse believes in attractiveness and you believe in modesty that could be a conflict. When people experience conflict, it is usually because their values are not aligned.

4. *Identify the top four values that your present job emphasizes.*

Are these values aligned with your values? Are there conflicts (be specific)?

Again we want to understand what the value conflicts are. If your job is staid and your employer is very traditional, and you strongly value variety, there is a conflict. If you value independence but your job emphasizes teamwork, that can be a conflict. Identifying your top values can help you get to the root of the situation, and understand what your main drivers are and whether these are aligned with your present job and employer.

5. *If you would choose a new job, what four values would you emphasize?*

Your answers to Question 4 will help you identify a new job you might want.

6. *What are the top four values of your mother, father or guardian?*

Are they aligned with your values? Are there conflicts (be specific)?

Often we don't stop think about how we develop the values we have. We don't consider how we were raised and how that contributes to who we are now. Some will fight against the values of their parents, and some gravitate toward them. Understanding your parents' values provides insights into the values you want in your partner and other important people in your life. If your parents emphasized frugality and you picked up this value, you will probably not gravitate toward someone who is extravagant. On the other hand, they may have been so frugal that you went in the opposite direction and value extravagance. If so, you want someone who likes to spend and not someone who is frugal.

7. *In thinking of your future goals, what four values should you adopt that you don't presently have?*

This is a great point of departure for how you may grow. Perhaps you want to be more thorough in the future, or be more timely because you tend to procrastinate. Or you were so independent you didn't share, and now you want to make sharing a future value. Or, you were meek, and now you want to emphasize persuasiveness. What do you want to change?

8. *What can you do to develop these values?*

When you reach the section about goals and objectives you will be able to elaborate more, but try to think now about what you can do to develop your desired values. You might decide to join a corporate sports team or be more vocal about issues at work. Brainstorm, but don't worry about pinning it down at this moment.

Chapter 4
Creating the Vision

Vision without action is a dream,
but action without vision is a nightmare.

Japanese proverb

1. Vision is insight turned into foresight

When a person begins to think about their values, they begin to think differently and use a very powerful tool -- visioning. With it, you can begin not just to think in new ways, but *see yourself* in new ways. Painter Vincent Van Gogh once said, "I dream my painting and I paint my dream." You too can begin to dream how your life will be, and then start to live that life.

Use *visioning* as a beginning step to start a journey into a life you can picture. It is an exercise that charts the change you wish to express. Ultimately, you can't *be better than you believe* unless you can create a new vision for your life's choices. Visioning is the beginning of a direction setting process which starts with identifying a vision or mission, and continues with specific goals and objectives to achieve that vision.

When one sets a vision, the vision is not based on what is, but what you want. A vision has the power to unleash your energy and your creative thought processes in a certain direction.

Almost every organizational entity sets up an annual budget, which outlines the allocation of monies and the deployment of resources. However, only excellent organizations also identify the vision and mission that will provide the context for these budgetary decisions. The process of visioning makes this a leadership action as opposed to just a management exercise. Setting the vision before the budget enables the organization to galvanize its creative forces and to imagine how it can perform better than it would have believed.

Visioning is not just the job of the most senior officer or the board of directors or trustees, but a process that involves all sectors of the organization, including input from key stakeholders, customers, clients, and constituencies, who now feel engaged in the organization in ways they may never have imagined. These key inputs (from inside and outside the organization) permit the organization to really drive change with a clear mandate.

Visioning also enables individuals and organizations to provide direction for their behavior, which typically leads to choices more thoughtful, deliberate, and effective than would be otherwise possible. Without visioning, organizations typically just make incremental adjustments, not the type of changes that may push them in a whole new direction. It provides a quality that can motivate, reinvigorate, and excite. It provides a quality that entities can aspire to.

It is all well and good to have management plans and budgets for the coming year. But an individual's or organization's behavior will not change just by setting goals, writing plans, or fine tuning the numbers, unless these activities are accompanied by a more far reaching process. Behavior changes only when an individual or organization goes through certain processes. Otherwise, they are destined to just do the same thing they were doing, year after year after year!

This process is the same for individuals as for organizations. How many times have you heard people state New Year's resolutions only to break them before the end of January? Usually the process of setting New Year's resolutions is like the annual rain dance. People go through the motions and hope for a dramatic outcome. When they don't get the dramatic outcome, then they go back to the same activities in which they were previously involved. A more deliberate effort is needed, which has greater efficacy and staying power.

Envisioning a new situation for yourself is empowering. It is exciting to imagine new possibilities that provide new opportunities to progress in your life, and liberating because, by visioning new possibilities, you shake yourself from the shackles that may be holding you back. You suddenly see opportunities where none existed before. This is because a vision sets the course or roadmap toward a brighter situation. Without this vision, it is impossible to set a roadmap because you don't know the direction in which you want to go. And if you don't know where you are going, then any road will take you there. You just keep doing the same thing and hope that it will make a difference. Hope does not make a difference unless it is followed by action. An old African proverb states, "When you pray, move your feet."

So what are the characteristics of a good vision?

2. The characteristics of good vision

a. Stretch statement

Visions are stretch statements that chart new paths. They move you along and help prevent you from repeating yourself. Albert Einstein once defined insanity as doing the same thing over and over again and expecting different results. If you keep doing the same thing, you will never move forward.

Examples: You say, "I want to lose five pounds" or, "I want to boost earnings 10 percent." These are statements, not visions. In fact, they are more dreams than anything else. A true vision stretches you so you do not repeat the same behavior year in and year out. Effective visions require you to perform differently.

For example, there is Sal, owner of a delicatessen in Brooklyn who sold traditional items, such as pastrami, turkey, ham, and cheese. In business for many years, Sal made a decent living. But one day he realized that, over the past few years, the neighborhood had changed with lots of residents from the West Indies. These folks were unfamiliar with pastrami, liverwurst and the like. They preferred their own cuisine.

Stores had already opened in the neighborhood offering food items that appealed more to the West Indian palate. Sal lived in the neighborhood, liked his neighbors who were very friendly, and did not want to move his business, prompting him to decide that, if his store were to survive, he would have to change. He researched West Indian cuisine and began offering prepared meals that included roti and curried goat. Rather than being a traditional delicatessen that offered foods people would cook or make into sandwiches, he developed a fairly sophisticated take-out service offering hot meals. It was a whole new vision of what his business offered customers, necessitated by his need to attract new customers. His business turned around and, at last report, was thriving.

The same thing holds true with large companies. Walt Disney Company was, for decades, associated with animated films and theme parks. Then it changed its vision and expanded its use of the Disney name. The new vision included retail stores and Broadway shows like "The Lion King" and "The Little Mermaid." The company developed in ways never before possible because it changed its vision.

b. Good vision involves others

When you communicate it to others, a number of things

happen. First, you are able to get more input and clarity that helps you to fine-tune your vision. Things always seem perfect in my mind, but when I articulate them to someone else, I am able to get clarity. What also happens is that when you involve others, it is no longer a secret. Involving others begins to invoke commitment because now someone else knows about it.

Furthermore, when you involve others, they can help by supporting you and offering advice to get closer to your vision. They may have suggestions that you wouldn't have thought of. They may know others who can help you. When you are progressing well they become your cheerleaders or your "amen corner," as I sometimes call it. We will discuss this more extensively in Chapter 7.

Let's face it -- making change is difficult, and you can use all the moral support you can muster. It is important to surround yourself with positive people who are good examples of what you are trying to achieve. Here, the importance of the company you keep is critical to getting what you want. Additionally, when you falter -- and we all do from time to time -- there is accountability because others know. Sometimes that voice in our head is not enough accountability to keep us honest and aligned with our vision.

Morris, a friend, was out of work and looking for a job. He was ashamed at being unemployed because he felt a stigma attached to being unemployed. For some time he didn't tell anyone he had lost his job, which meant no one could help him. This is a classic example of the saying, "you can't get different results without doing something different."

After a while, it became apparent to his friends that he was unemployed. When he realized others knew, he got the courage talk about it. He told friends and acquaintances that, while he wanted to stay in marketing, the field where he had spent his entire career, his goal was to move from the consumer products industry, where he had always worked, into the entertainment industry, where he had no experience. He needed to be more proactive to get a different result. His behavior of not talking about his situation was unproductive. According to the U.S. Bureau of Labor Statistics, over 70% of jobs are obtained through networking. Hence using family and friends expands your resources and improves your ability to connect to the position that you want.

The people he spoke to enrolled in his vision. At their suggestion, he moved from New York to Los Angeles, where friends and family helped him make the connections. He eventually was referred to a group of people who had great connections in the entertainment industry. They gave him feedback on what he needed to do to sharpen how he was selling himself, and after a number of interviews over several months, got a marketing job in the entertainment industry. It was a dream job, and it would never have come about had he not engaged others in his vision.

Often a CEO will state the vision for a company, especially, when the CEO is new to the job, only to learn such statements are not enough. For the CEO's vision to have any traction within the organization, employees must buy into it and adopt it as their own. Effective CEOs know this and work to engage everyone in the organization in their vision.

c. Goal alignment

For everyone to get behind a vision requires effort. Companies, for example, could set up one- or two-day offsite sessions where the vision statement is communicated, employees have an opportunity to provide input, and the effects of the vision statement are discussed. Such meetings help employees identify ways the vision will help them in their jobs and enhance their contribution to the organization. This is a way to instill the vision statement as part of each employee's vision, and not just as a directive upper management has forced down through the organization.

Suppose a company decided to open two new product categories a year on a global basis. When the individuals in the Latin American, Asian, and European divisions receive this vision, they begin to talk about how they could make it relevant to their part of the world and what resources they needed to achieve this vision. They discuss not just marketing, but research and development and manufacturing.

The organization knows that achieving the vision in a global corporation requires employees around the world to align the strategy to their objectives and goals. Their products and processes must be included. An American-based corporation cannot just tell its employees in other parts of the world to sell products identical to those sold in the U.S. The people, the products, and the processes must be reworked for local economies and cultures. This is a process that excellent companies undergo continually.

The most difficult aspect of the visioning process is getting buy-in and commitment up, down, and across the organization. Many organizations just have the chief executive and maybe the boards of directors develop platitudinous vision statements and credos, and then post them on the bulletin board, website, and company newsletter. They may even have a wooden plaque in the reception area. These are nice, but they don't evoke commitment. In fact, after a few months, nobody remembers them. They may even put the vision or mission statement on the company stationery and have it projected at the beginning of the annual meeting. These are good, but it will not make an organization great.

Needed is a process that involves as many people as practically possible and aligns them to the vision. What does involvement mean? Of course, it's not cost effective or even sensible to have everyone in the organization go to an offsite meeting. However, the key decision making figures for each organizational unit should meet and discuss how the vision will work in their area. They should articulate their own departmental or functional mission based on the corporate vision or mission. Then they should decide how to set and modify their specific departmental or functional objectives and goals based on that vision.

Individual contributors should ensure that their performance goals specify how they will execute the vision and implement the goals. In this way, the organization ensures that there is alignment between what they are doing, and the overall direction of the organization. Excellent organizations engage in this exercise annually before the budget process so that they ensure the vision drives the budget and not the other way around.

Goal alignment can be done in the family unit also at the beginning of the year, or at another appropriate watershed point. Naturally, you have to be practical in this process also. It makes sense to review your fixed, obligatory expenses first to see how you can meet those commitments. You have to decide on housing expenses, car payment, food, and other mandatory expenses. Your visioning process will have you review these items and other expenditures based on what you are trying to do.

For example, you may decide as part of your vision you want a new house in a different neighborhood. You may have to modify your present discretionary expenses in order to make this happen. You may also have to get a new job or promotion that pays more. Perhaps it is more realistic to get a condo instead of a house as an interim step. Or you may rent a less expensive apartment or not go on extravagant vacations for two to three years in order to satisfy your vision. There are lots of options, but certainly your finances and vision are intertwined and your process has to ensure they are aligned. I believe it is important to have a new vision every three years. This doesn't mean that you make drastic changes every three years, but it does mean you review your vision statement to see what needs to be modified.

d. Good vision energizes and excites.

A good vision excites people; it is something new and something to look forward to. Individuals don't get excited by doing the same thing every year. New visions chart out new directions that keep people motivated. Think about what happened when President Barack Obama announced his family would obtain a new dog. The Obama family was, of course, energized, but so was the public. The family's vision with this new household member touched millions.

A marriage where individuals come together for the first time in a new household needs a new vision also. Two independent individuals now have to be dependent. It is exciting to the new couple, but it is also exciting for everyone who knows and cares about them. A launch of a new product with a profound impact on the market breeds excitement. The company expects to grow and new opportunities begin to emerge for those inside the company. Employees expect to have new career moves within the organization. Such excitement is contagious. When individuals are associated with people who have grasped the new vision, they get excited.

You know you have a good vision when it provokes new

behavior and the expectation that things will change for the better. In the public arena, this is why words like leadership and innovation have so much traction. People expect leaders will provide new direction and inject new thoughts. They expect leaders will bring new ideas to the table through their vision. Innovation triggers the same spark in people. Innovation implies something new, such as new products or services or ways of accomplishing tasks. These are expected to perform better than what was there. The human psyche often yearns for this freshness and novelty.

3. How do you set up a vision and put it into action?

Break down your vision into actionable statements you can implement and act upon. The vision statement is followed by objectives and goals, which are highly specific. You specify objectives first, and then the goals to achieve each of those objectives. Many organizations use the words mission and vision interchangeably. They also use the words objective and goal interchangeably. The best way to determine whether a statement will be a vision, which is a broader concept, or a goal, which is more specific, is to ask *"how"* and *"why"* questions.

Let's say you have a statement: We will build a new train line (this is currently happening in New York City with the Second Avenue subway on Manhattan's East Side). Is this a vision or objective? You need to ask: Why are we going to build a subway line? The answer might be because you want to provide greater geographic access for individuals traveling from one point to another. The vision of the new subway line is that it will provide greater access for people to travel on the East Side. Now we can have a "How" statement, which includes specific goals to achieve the vision. The objective might be: Complete four miles of the line by 2014. This is an objective -- a goal -- not a vision. The vision provides the people of New York with the wherewithal to more easily traverse Manhattan's East Side.

Another example: You head a small bank and want to install an additional 50 ATM's (automatic teller machines). Is this a vision statement or a goal? It is a goal. The vision behind it is the desire to give consumers greater convenience to access their money.

The bank's vision may be to become the number one provider for all the financial needs of its customers. How it achieves that involves objectives and goals. The "How "might go beyond installing more ATMs and include expanding product offerings, such as mortgages, credit cards, business loans, and insurance. This can also apply to large banks. Citibank had the vision to be the sole provider of financial services to its customers (its vision) and acquired the brokerage firm, Smith Barney and the insurance company, Travelers, to achieve this vision.

On an individual basis, say your vision is to play the trumpet. Playing a trumpet is not necessarily a vision statement because there may be another reason behind it. You might in fact want to have a new hobby, and that would be your vision statement and learning to play the trumpet would be part of your goals. Or your vision is to become very knowledgeable about music, and playing the trumpet is a means to that end. The old vision: Learn to play the trumpet. The new vision: Get a new hobby or learn about music. That is why you need to ask "Why" questions. Use this approach to prompt you to understand your vision and to look at different goals and objectives to achieve your vision.

Can I see the vision?

Many people see *visioning* as a frivolous exercise. Thoughts come to mind of people running in the forest or on the beach, or sitting in hot tubs and chanting. These exercises have their place and may make you feel good, but they don't provoke change, or so some folks think. It is extremely important to articulate a vision and then follow up with specific objectives and goals that can be measured.

Let us take this a step further with the individual vision. Suppose you have a vision of wanting a new home. This may be a good vision, but it needs a lot more body in order to be achievable. The objective may be to get a three bedroom home in a warm climate, with good schools and favorable cost of living. Several objectives must be accomplished to bring this about. For example, you may have to reduce your discretionary spending.

How do you reduce your discretionary spending? This gets you into defining more specific goals. You may have to take one vacation instead of two each year. You may be able to eat out only once a month, instead of five times. Holiday spending for gifts may have to be limited to $50 a person instead $100, and reserved for immediate family only. At this stage of objectives and goals, be specific and quantify the items. Being specific makes them more achievable. You want to work on something that is tangible, not amorphous.

Measuring your results is critical because this enables you to see whether you are really engaged in efforts that will achieve your vision, or whether you are defeating your efforts. One of the major reasons why people do not achieve their vision is because they don't have a way of monitoring their progress. When you only have a vision, without objectives and goals, then you cannot determine whether you are on target or not. Furthermore, there is no way to determine how to make mid-course corrections to get back on track. This is the beauty of not going through the process piecemeal. While organizations may create objectives and goals as a normal part of their process, individuals aren't always as comprehensive and thorough. An old adage states, "What gets measured gets done." This is certainly the case when it comes to visioning efforts.

4. Can your vision open up new possibilities?

You have to ask "How "and "Why "questions to find out whether your vision is correct. Example: British Air stated it wanted to be the premiere British airline carrying business-class passengers between New York and Paris (yes, Paris). This was the vision. The implementation was developing a new airline called OpenSkies that catered only to business travelers going between New York and Paris. Who knows where that vision will take OpenSkies in the future? A vision statement, if you go through the right process, opens a whole new set of options for you. Ask how-else or what-else questions to open up possibilities and options. How else can we transport passengers between New York and Paris? Where else will they offer business class service? What other new services can be offered for business and first class flyers?

I knew a restaurant owner in a small New Jersey town who wanted to offer haute cuisine at affordable prices. This town is known for having excellent restaurants. However, to provide affordable haute cuisine or gourmet cuisine to families, he decided to start a delivery service and not a retail restaurant, where he would deliver meals to the home and set up the person's table with disposable silverware and glasses. This was an innovative concept that came from his vision of offering gourmet cuisine at affordable prices. And it worked. The business quickly became successful.

A new vision provides businesses the opportunities to branch into new services and individuals to develop new capabilities and competencies. The restaurant owner had to decide whether he wanted to specialize in great fast delivery, or affordable haute cuisine. You could see all type of possibilities depending on which distinctive competency he wanted to emphasize. That is a strategic choice. We will talk more about this in the chapter on branding, but it is critical to stay "close to your knitting." That is, to stick with what you do best and which aligns with your distinctive competencies.

New capabilities and competencies open the door to execute your vision effectively. There is no way to *be better than you believe* without having a vision that charts the new direction of change. In the next chapter, let's look at the role that distinctive competencies play.

Thought Stimulators

Ask yourself:

1. *What is your personal ultimate vision statement?*

This is a wonderful exercise because it helps you understand what you really want. You may want to move to a warm location that may be less stressful. Or you are single and you want to have a spouse and several children. You may want to start your own business. Looking into the future, how do you want yourself to be?

2. *What are the three goals needed to achieve that vision?*

(Use "How" and "Why" questions as illustrated earlier to distinguish what your vision is from the goals to achieve it.)

Let's say your ultimate vision is to move to a warm climate. How will you achieve that? Start by first identifying areas of the country or world with the characteristics you want. Clarify whether you can get a job at these locations. Consider whether this move is worth leaving you personal support system and/ or family relationships where you currently are. The "Why" questions will get you to your ultimate vision and the "How" will facilitate moving toward that vision.

3. What is your ultimate organizational vision?

What are the three goals needed to achieve that vision? (Use "How" and "Why" statements to distinguish your vision from your goals.) Let's say you own a midsized business and want to expand into global markets. How do you do that? You would identify countries likely to be receptive to your products and services. You could also look for others suitable as joint-venture partners. In addition, you might hire someone who understands the culture, language and economics of where you want to go. This a good way to identify "How" and "Why" questions.

Or, suppose you want to sell your products through the Internet. Of course, you need a website. To achieve this, you can hire a consultant or website design firm, or take the job in-house and hire an employee with the technical know-how and marketing savvy to sell online. Again the "How" and "Why" questions will get you closer to not just what you want to do, but how you achieve it.

Chapter 5
Identifying Your Distinctive Competencies

*In jazz, hierarchy is determined by your ability to play,
not your position in the band.*

Wynton Marsalis

1. **Rediscovering who you want to be, not what you want
   to do**

Outlining one's vision – whether an individual's or an organization's -- is really the starting point for renewal. Formulating
a vision is an opportunity to reassess not just what we want
to do, but who we want to be. Think of a vision statement
as a tool that helps a person or organization understand their
unique contribution and what they are good at doing.

It is critical, after you create your vision, to decide whether
it is in line with your capabilities.

I may have a vision to be an opera singer, but there are a

few things that make this highly impracticable. While I love to sing, I have zero ability to sing in tune. Further, even if I learn how to sing in key as a tenor, I will never be able to reach the octave levels required of a serious virtuoso. Additionally, when I think about the areas that coincide with my strengths, singing would not be among them. You need a reality test for your visioning efforts, and identifying your distinctive competencies helps you to focus and fine tune your efforts.

Consider the story of Theodore, who upon finishing law school and practicing law for a few years, decided he didn't like the law. Instead, he wanted to be a mediator and practice internationally to capitalize on his facility with languages and desire to travel. The day-to-day humdrum of writing briefs and appearing in court that characterized his law career were unappealing.

He took an inventory of his distinctive competencies, and devised a vision of his professional life based on them. He was good at mediating disputes -- in fact, mediation was what drew him to the law in the first place – so he made this his focus. Also, he spoke Spanish and French fluently and liked to travel, which made sense for him to work internationally. He loved learning new languages and the experiences associated with speaking in different tongues. And he felt he had entrepreneurial abilities. Being able to call his own shots and create his own business was appealing and used his distinctive competencies better than if he stayed in law and became a partner in a law firm.

Once completing his inventory, he set into motion a plan to realize his vision. Asia-Pacific was the geographic area that most appealed to him. When an undergraduate, he studied Chinese and also had relatives on the West Coast. To more easily address this region, he moved from New York to San Diego to be closer to his target market, and set up a consulting firm. Previously, he worked with the State Department, and when he set up his own shop, the State Department agreed to let him handle a mediation dispute in the Philippines. The end result: Theodore's consulting firm, which focused on mediating trade disputes in the Asia-Pacific region, got off to a great start and became highly successful. You can see how Theodore was able to go with his strengths, but focus on another way of capitalizing on his distinctive capabilities.

Another person making a change was Linda, a Midwest attorney by training. Linda went to Los Angeles because her dream was to become an entertainment agent. When in college, where Linda minored in music, she interned in Los Angeles and made a lot of connections in the music and acting industries, which she cultivated over the years, never knowing where they might lead. Her connections and networking have now paid off, and last we spoke, her agent business was doing well.

Theodore and Linda are not my only lawyer acquaintances who found the law did not capitalize on their distinctive competencies. In fact, I have several friends in this industry who enjoy it immensely. Some, however, have not taken advantage of their distinctive competencies and have remained in

◄ BEING BETTER THAN YOU BELIEVE

the legal profession – and are noticeably dissatisfied with their professional development. Sometimes the area you originally start out in -- whether it is law, medicine, business, social work or teaching -- does not allow you to fully use your capabilities. This is where creativity is required to make other applications of your skills, while still staying close to your "knitting."

When individuals are really getting closer to who they want to be, it helps to not just look at one's job, profession, or employer, but also to think about how to execute the competencies that make them distinctive. Virtually everyone has distinctive competencies, and they are where you should place your focus.

2. The Head-and-Shoulders Test

To determine what are your distinctive competencies, consider areas where you are head-and-shoulders above others. I call this the *Head-and-Shoulders test* or HST. Which of your competencies really stand out in a distinctive way and make you shine among people who do what you do?

I use printing companies to produce my marketing materials. People think all printing companies are practically the same and what distinguishes them is only price and access to different types of materials such as paper stock. Gino owns a printing company, and easily passes the HST. His prices are competitive but not always the lowest. He has access to lots of paper stock and can do various fancy printing techniques, but

◄ 102

so can many other printing companies.

Gino's distinctive competency: customer service. He always keeps me updated with the progress of a project. As with any other printer, sometimes a job runs late. When this happens, he lets me know and gives me the new deadline. I do not have to call and ask for the job; he anticipates my need and calls before I have a chance. He is always cordial. Even if I call after business hours, he will typically get back to me within three or four hours. Customer service is extremely important to me. That's why I use Gino even if he costs a little bit more.

Another example involves a coffeehouse chain. Where I live in Manhattan, I have no shortage of conveniently located coffeehouses. But I go to one shop almost every time because they make my chai latte exactly the way I like it. They put the ingredients together in just the right way. The other coffeehouses in the area always produce a chai latte that falls short of the mark when it comes to my personal taste. The one I frequent -- which also typically seems more crowded than the others -- passes the HST.

I have attended succession planning meetings at large companies. Here, senior managers review members of their teams and decide who are the best candidates to become future leaders in the organization. The capabilities and potential of team members are discussed, and those with leadership potential are identified. Positions in the organization that need to be filled are listed and then matched with individuals who seem best able to fill those positions. These future leaders are given the opportunity to move around the organization to learn more about the business, are given management and leadership training, and provided with increasing responsibilities.

Identifying the right person can be tricky. For example, when moving a marketing person to a general-manager position, you look for different capabilities than those that made the person successful in the first place. A good marketing person might be adept at new product development, or writing advertising, or executing promotion plans. But a general manager needs distinct characteristics that demonstrate not just an ability to be creative and to execute, but be able to lead and manage people.

To determine who has such capabilities, the succession meeting focuses on a person's overall competencies to see if they have what it takes not just to be a good marketing person, but also a senior managing director. Also it is important to identify those competencies distinctive to the new position. This may mean requiring abilities related to communication, strategic planning, and managing large, complex departments.

Identifying your competencies requires an understanding of what distinguishes you from others in your profession. In what ways do you stand head-and-shoulders above your peers? What are your unique attributes? Sometimes, however, the impression we have of ourselves is not the same as the impression others have of us. This disconnect I will now discuss.

3. Do others know what you want them to know about you?

Our self impressions are often very different than those others have of us, and this is arguably the biggest problem we have when communicating. I did an exercise with two individuals who worked in information technology, Warren and Constantine, who had known each other for more than five years. I asked Warren what areas he thought Constantine was more skilled in -- which were his most distinctive competencies. And then I asked Constantine the same thing about himself.

Warren said Constantine was professional but also very technically proficient. Constantine's self-identified distinctive competencies were being thorough and helpful. Note, there is a slight disconnect here. "Thorough and helpful" is not quite the same as "professional." Warren didn't value helpfulness as much as Constantine, while Constantine felt that being helpful to people and going to the ends of the earth to solve people's problems was his major strength. Such disconnects between how we view ourselves and how others view us are very, very common.

Jean and Dolores worked together in human resources. I asked Jean about Dolores's strongest area, and she said Dolores was a really hard worker and that is what she valued the most. But when I asked Dolores what were her strengths, being a team builder and good communicator was what she said.

These disconnects exist because individuals don't always see themselves in the way others see them. If Dolores wants to be known as a team builder and good communicator and not just a hard worker, what can she do to be seen in this way? Two psychologists developed a model that assists in this. Joseph Luft and Harry Ingram developed the Johari Window to help individuals understand how to get to a more balanced point between how you see yourself and how others do.

Essentially they state that when things are known to an individual and to others, it is called the *Arena* because they share this knowledge in common. For example, I can see you have a nice blue tie and you can see it also. No question about it. Next are those items known to others, but not known to you. This represents your *Blind Spot.* Continuing with the previous example, there may be a grease stain on your tie that others can see, but you can't unless someone makes it known to you. Then there are items that are known to you, but not to others. This is your *Façade,* which is what you are not revealing. Again, it may be that you have another tie of a different color in your pocket, but you have not revealed it yet. Then there are items that are unknown to you and others which are called the *Unknown.*

To get to the *Arena* where what you and others know about you are common, seek feedback from others or use opportunities to provide more disclosure. This enables you to move closer to the *Arena* and eliminate issues that come from you and others not having a shared understanding.

For example, to find out what others identify as your distinctive competencies, write down the three words you think best describe yourself. Then ask colleagues: What are the three words you would use to describe me? If your three words are different than those used by others, you have a disconnect, and need to work on closing that gap.

A further challenge is that in our world, we often don't use three words. Today, that seems long. Often we speak in what I call "short speak" -- one or two words that describe the unique aspects of a person's contribution. In management meetings, I'll ask about an individual and I'll get back one-word descriptions: resourceful, stubborn, arrogant, a nitpicker, intelligent.

Whether long-speak or short-speak, the issue is whether or not the image others have of you aligns with the message you want to get across. Are they seeing you the way you want to be seen?

Recently I had a first-hand experience in this area. I was a speaker at an event, and the person making my introduction said I was a good communicator. Now, I view myself as a good communicator, so this comment was not off base, but it was too limited. I had hoped he would say I was good communicator who had a global perspective. That may not sound important to some, but in my consulting work, my international experience is one of my distinctive competencies, and this was not obvious to the other person who was introducing me. I have been introduced at other meetings where my global experience was mentioned in my introduction. At that particular meeting, I had to spend some of the time during my talk discussing my global mindset to let the audience know about this distinctive competency. They get it now! It is always important to consider how your competencies are distinctive so you add value whenever you go.

4. Developing your competitive edge

Individuals need to determine what areas distinguish them over others and what might be missing when they communicate their distinctive competencies to others. Develop your competitive edge by having a good understanding of not only what is important to you, but to your clients and key stakeholders. When you really understand what your audience needs, see if you can develop the competency required to fill that need.

An example is Carlos, a finance person who worked for a company that wanted to develop more business in emerging world markets. Carlos found that many in his department lacked an understanding of hyperinflation accounting and finance. This is managing a company's accounting and finance functions when in an economy with inflation of 30 to 50 percent a year or more, and the country's currency is being devalued just about every single day. Over the last 15 years, we have seen such hyperinflation in Zimbabwe, Argentina, Turkey, and Russia, among other countries.

Carlos thought he could distinguish himself in the developing BRIC countries. This competency would put him head-and-shoulders over virtually everyone else he would compete with. He saw the gap -- the need of companies to have someone knowledgeable in hyperinflation accounting and finance -- and was willing to learn that competency to fill the gaps companies had in their internal abilities.

He was also open to moving his family, since learning such skills required him to move. Though born in the Dominican Republic, Carlos took positions in both Russia and Turkey to learn more about those economies. His colleagues, though, were unwilling to move and to learn hyperinflation skills, and stayed in the Western European countries. As a result, the trajectory of Carlos's career went much faster and higher in the organization than his colleagues'.

Another friend, Bob, was a budding IT professional. The insight he had was that in the IT world, desktop publishing would become very important. With his employer, he was unable to find a position where he could learn desktop publishing. Though he had a good job, he decided to take a chance and moved to Silicon Valley to work at a startup company. Building from this position, where he learned a great deal about desktop publishing, he then moved to a job at Apple, and eventually started his own desktop publishing enterprise with several others, all of whom learned their IT skills at Stanford. Desktop publishing was an area where he saw a need and felt he could really distinguish himself. He was right and has been able to progress very well.

Bob and Carlos distinguished themselves from their colleagues, and in so doing, rose head-and-shoulders above them. When identifying your distinctive competencies, focus not just on what is needed, but also on your own sweet spot.

5. What is your sweet spot?

Tennis players look for the sweet spot of a racket, which allows them to hit the ball with precision or power or spin. People can hit the ball a number of different ways, but if they hit on the racket's sweet spot, they are more likely to hit accurately and get an ace.

The same holds true of people and businesses, which have products, services, or abilities that really make a difference. I go to Nathan's Hot Dogs, a fast food chain that has something of a national presence, but is a New York institution. Nathan's has great hot dogs. But what I really go there for is their French fries that, by my reckoning, are the best of any fast food chain. I don't go to certain fried chicken chains for their mashed potatoes or fish; I go for their fried chicken. Some companies try to be all things to all people, and suffer as a result. The same with people -- you cannot pass the HST in all areas. If you are highly competent in only one or two areas, you are still ahead of the competition

I spoke before a group of community college leaders who wanted to improve their colleges' ability to attract students. My message to them was: Find what you are better at than other colleges. Are you more conveniently located? Are you more nurturing, which results in a higher graduation rate? Are you focused on particular populations, such as certain ethnic groups or nationalities? Do you have strength catering to the needs of local businesses, such as having a strong IT department in a city with lots of high tech companies? You, too, need to understand your strengths and capitalize on them.

Even colleges that offer a wide variety of curriculum are often known for particular areas. One person I know wants to study for a Ph.D. in anthropology with a focus on cultural anthropology. A number of schools offer such a focus, but only a handful of schools stand out. Students from around the world go to these universities just to study cultural anthropology.

Let me give you one more example of a sweet spot. If I fly from New York to say Kansas City, I fly Midwest airlines. In fact, any chance I get to use this airline, I do because they treat every seat like a business class-seat. These are sweet spots that are critical to my choice of air carriers. Finding a sweet spot helps you become more than you believe you can be.

6. Find the gap

You can always identify a gap that exists and fill it. You can always chart your own path. Do you think that weathermen and women are all alike? I watch the weather report every morning to see what I should wear during the day. Weather reporting is a very interesting but inexact science, though still important to me. When I watch NBC, Al Roker reports the national weather broadcast. A good weatherman, I also find he is comical, personable and provides great entertainment value through his jokes and one-liners. He gives the weather report like others, but let's face it, I want to be entertained in the morning because, often, the news is very grim. Al's sweet spot is humor and it gets me through the day's rain or shine. Al has found the gap.

Do you think you have to wait until you are older to identify your distinctive competencies? Definitely not! When students apply to colleges, they have to identify at least one critical sweet spot that helps them stand out from among their peers. What is the one thing they need to clarify that will make the admissions department select them? Every student is told to get involved in community activities and demonstrate some extra curricula involvement. However, even better is demonstrating their ability to lead a community activity.

Lorenzo decided to become involved in tutoring inner city youth in Chicago. However, the group, the South Side Tutoring Group, had already chosen a president. So what did Lorenzo do? He set up a committee that focused on the math component of the tutoring effort, and became head of this group. By doing so, he was able demonstrate leadership even though the top position was filled.

Always find the gap. Always chart a new path to demonstrate distinctive competence. Lorenzo found the gap and I am sure in part because of it, was accepted to the University of Massachusetts.

Joan wanted her application to shine also. All of her friends went on trips to Europe and were involved in varsity sports in high school. They played tennis, track and field, gymnastics etc. Joan wanted to attend the University of Minnesota because of its turf grass science program. Yes, that's right, turf grass science, a unique specialty, but they offer it at the University of Minnesota and that is their distinctive competence. What caught the eye of the admission committee at the university: Joan's being captain of the girls' ice hockey team in high school.

When Bryan completed his undergraduate work at the City University of New York, he wanted to go into a graduate business program. Almost every business graduate school applicant knows you need two to three years of serious work experience in order to make his or her graduate application attractive so he decided to go into investment banking. The market is flooded with students who went into investment banking, making investment banking resumes fairly commonplace. Bryan had a challenge to stand out and decided to not only go into investment banking, but do so in Johannesburg, where he could engage in business development throughout southern Africa. This gave him an edge over his competitors.

7. Identify and communicate

Individuals must walk the talk. If you say you want to be a caring person, do individuals actually see you as such a person? If you say you want to be a good listener, are you really a good listener? Some people display strengths that vary according to the setting they are in. They display certain abilities at home but not at work, or vice versa. They might display a characteristic to their supervisor but not their peers or subordinates.

I use a multi-rater coaching process called 360 degree coaching to get multiple levels of feedback regarding an individual's behavior. In this process I ask participants to get their subordinates, peers, and supervisors to give them feedback about their abilities and competencies in certain areas. Invariably, they find they are seen differently by peers, supervisors, and subordinates -- and their self concept often differs from all three of these to a degree. What I usually do is coach the individual to understand the disconnect between his or her self concept with those of significant others. Then I help them engage in activities to change their behavior to bridge the gap in perception.

In many cases, the individual has to communicate differently, engage differently, and interact differently. Little things can really be big things. I have stayed at the W Hotel in Atlanta and what most impressed me was that when I leave in the morning and return at night, the cleaning attendants give me a cheerful good morning and good evening greeting. I spend about 50 percent of my time in hotels, and rarely do cleaning attendants say anything to me. Such greetings are little things but leave big impressions. You might say to me to get a life, but how was your last hotel stay? In fact, the W Hotel has done a number of things to make them head and shoulders over the competition. They pioneered an extra fluffy pillow-top bed and also the rounded rods in the bathroom tub. They invested quite a bit to get this competitive advantage and now many other hotels have copied them. The greeting, however, is distinctive. You can't copy good manners; you just have to believe it and make it part of your DNA.

I flew Virgin America from New York to San Francisco, and what impressed me was that the pilot, before he sat down in the cockpit, introduced himself over the public address system and wished us a good flight. And when he got into his seat, he gave his name again. I will fly them again because there is a human being in the cockpit who seems to care. Compare this to a cab company I will not name. The company's slogan: We serve. I had three pieces of luggage and they didn't help me load or unload my luggage from their cab. Slogans don't make it. Actions do.

8. What got you there may not keep you there

Whatever your situation, you usually find there are other competencies you will have to develop to gain staying power and move up in the organization. For example, technical skills, such as those needed by IT, finance, and medical professionals, can get you there. But what got you there may not keep you there unless you develop additional distinctive competencies, such as leadership and management abilities.

Sam was an excellent finance person who was promoted because he was able to introduce new methods for cost saving and increase profitability in difficult regions of the world.

Based on these successes, he was promoted to managing director of a subsidiary of a large company. And what will keep him there is an ability to develop a management team and demonstrate his expertise in a number of functional areas other than finance, such as marketing research and development, and manufacturing. For him to continue moving up, he must provide not just a finance perspective, but develop strategies that make everybody feel a part of the team. He worked on those areas where he was weak, and as a result got promoted to head a countrywide division of a fairly large country. He showed he was not just a good finance person, but a good managing director.

9. How do I get that promotion?

Let's put some of the previous thoughts together and talk about how you can use your distinctive competencies to get promoted. There is one very basic flaw that too many people have in organizations. They feel that if they are on the job long enough, doing what they consider to be a good work, a promotion and raise will be automatic. While this may hold for certain positions, it does not hold overall anymore.

Jonathan worked for over 25 years as an administrative assistant for communications and media company. He rarely got sick. He was accurate with his work and received excellent ratings. He went to the human resources department several times and told them he wanted to be promoted into management and receive a higher grade level. He even went back to school at night to get a master's degree in business.

The promotion still eluded him until he changed his strategy. The issue was that he needed to demonstrate he had project management skills and also team building capability. These were the primary competencies required for the next position in management. He needed an opportunity to demonstrate these capabilities and then sell himself differently for the job. His primary tactic before was just to say that he had been with the company for 25 years and that he did a good job, which was indicated by his ratings, and that this should be enough to get him promoted. This clearly was not the case.

After he received coaching, he asked his supervisor to involve him in a project that would improve file retention and put on microfiche a number of paper documents. This project took about a year, but through it he was able to show he could manage projects and coordinate the efforts of the entire department administrative cadre. Furthermore, he was able to provide timely reports to management on the progress and at the end of the project was able to show a savings of 25% in fixed expenses.

He didn't say anything about a promotion until after he finished the project, but was able to clearly present a different rationale showing his value to the company. He was able to show he had the competencies of not only the present job, but those needed for the position he aspired to. He did get promoted as a result, but it was because he was able to demonstrate he had what it took to perform in the next position.

This is the key to promoting yourself differently. All too often people think that because they do a good job, this automatically prepares them for the next position. It is critical to be able to identify the capailities of the next position, and then to demonstrate how you are able to perform those skills.

The best way to position yourself, though, is to seek out opportunities to actually show you are able to do what it is that the next level up requires. Nothing speaks better than having the evidence you can do a job because you have performed certain aspects of the role. You will have to go above and beyond your present position, but doing so speaks volumes when you want to sell yourself differently.

This is even the case when you are looking to move to another company. Some interviewers are very good and some are not. No matter what they do, you should always focus on activities and projects you were involved in that demonstrate your application of the required competencies. You are in a stronger position when you can articulate not only what you will do, but to give specific examples that demonstrate some of the skills the job requires.

Usually when you are going into a new position or seeking a new role at another company, it involves positioning your distinctive competencies in a very strategic manner. This has to do with how you brand and rebrand yourself. This will enable you to be better than you believe and we will discuss this in the next chapter.

Thought Stimulators

Ask yourself:

1. What are your three most distinctive competencies?

In order to achieve your vision, you need the knowledge, skills, and capabilities to do what you want to do: I sum this up as a competency. What's important about a competency is being as specific as you can. For example, if you say one of your competencies is leadership, you must be able to take the initiative, be proactive, and have foresight that you can put into action. Some individuals will say one of their competencies is they are a "people person." I cringe when I hear this because it doesn't give any detail. If they say they are a good listener, relate well to others, and are able to communicate their points without ambiguity, this gets a little closer to a "people person" competency.

2. When considering your vision and goals, which of these competencies fit the Head-and-Shoulders Test (i.e., really make you shine among your peers)?

If you say you are a people person and can outline what aspects of that competency really make you shine, then you will be head-and-shoulders above others. Some are good at talking and getting their point across, but are not good listeners. In my experience, many CEOs are good talkers and communicate their points well, but I have found many often don't listen well. Listening is a competency that puts you head-and-shoulders above your peers. If a leader is also sensitive to the needs of his or her constituency, that puts him head-and-shoulders above his peers. How often have you heard individuals say someone is smart? Being smart is not good enough, especially if there are other smart people around.

3.   *Do the litmus test for your personal competencies:*

Describe yourself in one sentence. Use action words and verbs.

Examples:

I have great ability to communicate well with individuals on a one-on-one basis.

I am considered a good listener. I have the ability to focus on the details.

4.   *Ask two people whose opinions you value to describe you in one sentence.*

- Is their view of you totally aligned with your self concept?

- What did you learn in this exercise that you didn't know about yourself?

- Is there a disconnect? If so, why do you think that is

the case?

This is important because we all have a view of ourselves and think we know ourselves well, but when we ask others what they think of us, we gain additional insights.

Are their views aligned with your concept of yourself? Are they saying something about you that you haven't highlighted, that you have ignored, or you weren't aware of in the first place?

Sometimes individuals can see something in us that we may have been reluctant to highlight. For example, some individuals put on a veneer of being strong and competent, but what also comes through is that the person is very sensitive, and they do not highlight this.

5. *Ask two people whose feedback you value, what you can do differently to behave closer to your original self concept.*

Let us say you want to demonstrate sensitivity, but are not sure how. Such feedback can give you clues on how to be perceived the way you want. Maybe you want to be considered proactive, but have not been able to demonstrate this. The feedback can help you demonstrate your proactive character.

Chapter 6
Initiating the Personal Rebranding Process

*To be yourself in a world that is trying to make you
something else is my greatest accomplishment.*

Ralph Waldo Emerson

Everybody has a personal brand

Usually people think of the concept of brand just in the marketing sense. However, thinking of a brand in relationship to your personal identity, whether individual or corporate, requires taking into account a number of other elements.

When we talk about personal brands, first consider how a brand is different than a product. What is a brand? What is a product? A product usually is a commodity item, for example, Coca-Cola and Pepsi-Cola. Both are sodas and beverages, and they come in bottles and cans. So how are they differentiated? "Elephants on Acid & Other Bizarre Experiments," a study cited by Alex Boese, conducted by Baylor School of Medicine provides insight on this. The experiment presented a panel of tasters with an unlabeled cola and one that they said was Coke. Over 85% of the panelists selected Coke over the unlabeled cola even though both colas were the same. This easily illustrates the effect that branding has on the choices that people make.

Coke's brand emphasizes its classic qualities, its position as a bedrock American icon known and respected globally. Coke is one of the greatest brand names of all time, and its product, the beverage itself, reflects this mainstream image. Pepsi's brand is different, connoting innovation, entertainment, and youthfulness. Because their brands are so different, consumers easily differentiate between the two products, despite the similarity between the products themselves. Branding is the differentiator.

Another example is Microsoft versus Apple. Ten years ago, if asked to describe these two companies, you probably would have said both are computer companies, with Microsoft being the more staid of the two and Apple the more youthful. The very name Apple is kind of playful and reflects the brand of the company.

But today, the branding of the two companies is more different than ever. Microsoft is still identified by its computer software products, such as Windows and Office. It has branched out into music players with its Zune MP3 player and video games with its line of Xbox players and games, but the company is still basically a computer software company.

Not so for Apple. Today, Apple is far more than just a maker of computer hardware and software. Revenues from its iPod MP3 music player and iPhone smart phone nearly equal those of its revenues from the Mac computer. The company revolutionized how music is distributed and listened to with its iPod and iTunes online music store. Then it shifted the market for smart phones with its innovative touch-screen iPhone. Then came the iPad, which made tablet computers more popular than ever. Music and cell phones are markets in which it had no presence a decade ago. Apple's brand has expanded from being innovative to being fun and entertaining, which previously did not apply to it -- nor do these words relate to Microsoft in most people's minds. Apple has, in effect, rebranded itself over the past several years, which is reflected in its dropping the word "computer" from its name; it was Apple Computer Inc. and is now Apple Inc.

Branding applies to people as well as products. Only over the last 10 years have we really begun to think of branding in this way; however, the concept has been around in a nascent form for several decades. When Senator John F. Kennedy was running for president of the United States against Vice President Richard Nixon in 1960, we witnessed a televised debate. The image of a young, vibrant, good looking, charismatic person debating a person who looked stern, determined, and no-nonsense left an indelible imprint on the minds of those who watched. Depending on your political persuasion, you would probably ascribe other adjectives to each of them. Many people probably were not consciously aware of why they voted the way they did in the presidential election, but certainly these images gave a sharp enough contrast for people to make a choice.

So the personal brand of the contestants was introduced in the mass media and became a key factor in determining who would be elected. The personal brand of President Kennedy from the standpoint of leadership and vision is noteworthy to many.

The proliferation of mass media and technological innovations in communication has put the personality of individuals to the forefront as never before. This causes us to look at the personality characteristics of public figures as never before. Have you noticed that whenever a new CEO is appointed to an organization, the press release announcing the appointment portrays the individual in a way that highlights his or her essential personal and leadership characteristics? It may have a picture of the person rowing a boat or hiking, or it might play up family characteristics and educational background. The hope is that by portraying these characteristics, people will feel comfortable with this person at the helm of the organization and have confidence he or she can create a better tomorrow.

What is the first thing a mother or father will say when a son or daughter is considering getting married? "What is he or she like? Do they fit in this family? Are they good enough for my son or daughter?" When students gather to register for college courses, they do not just want to know the topic of the course, they want to know about the professor.

Consider the actors Denzel Washington and Russell Crowe. Both are very good at what they do, but their brands are different. Crowe is intense, mercurial, and even a bit rough-and-tumble. Washington's brand is more courtly, and includes a high degree of integrity, as well as good physical looks.

When talking about people, a person's brand personifies their distinctive competencies. Washington is able to portray staid and cool characters, while Crowe is good at portraying intense and physical characters. When you understand your distinctive competencies, you can begin to personify them as a brand that reflects the range of your capabilities and values. I could go on and on, but you get the point. How one is branded matters.

Whether we realize it or not, we all have a brand. Each of us is known for something, just as each of us has distinctive competencies. We may not always be aware of our brand, but when others think of us, our brand is what they attribute to us. Which raises the question: What do we want our brand to be? If we are going to be better than we believe, we have to think about how we will rebrand ourselves and change how we are positioned to improve our performance, improve our standing, and achieve new goals.

When we identify our change proposition, outline our new vision, and clarify our distinctive competencies, we have an opportunity to rebrand.

When and why rebrand

There are a number of reasons to consider rebranding. First, when you have identified your vision, your vision in and of itself begins to chart a new direction for you. But you cannot just proceed in that new direction by doing the same things you always did. You have to consider how to do things differently. To capitalize on new opportunities, you need to determine what you must do differently. After outlining your vision, then you want to review your values and what needs to be adjusted to fit the new vision.

Identifying your distinctive competencies sets the foundation for your new brand. Some people may start by branding themselves first, and then identifying the competencies that fit. The process is certainly more cyclical than linear, but you must make sure there is alignment and fit between your brand and your capabilities to execute the brand effectively. If your distinctive competencies do not provide a means for you to express your brand, you will never be successful. Your brand becomes only a pipedream.

Sally, for example, was a global marketing director who worked in several countries, always as the head of marketing. And when a promotion was available, it too was as a head of marketing in some country or region. Sally wanted to expand her opportunities beyond marketing, and start on a career path that would lead to becoming a managing director of a large subsidiary of a major corporation. In such a position, she would supervise not just marketing, but sales, finance, human resources, information technology, and manufacturing.

To rebrand herself as managing director material, first she identified her distinctive competencies. She realized she would have to expand those competencies to show she understood finance, distribution, and the like, so she began to spend more time with the finance people to demonstrate her understanding of the cost structure of products.

Often, marketing people lack a detailed understanding of the businesses' material costs, distribution costs, inventory costs, and discount allowances. When creating product promotions, they may not be concerned with the effect of their decisions on inventory, warehousing, and storage costs. Hence, a lot of slow moving, obsolete products may result, putting a burden on the overall cost structure. This ties up capital and limits the company's ability to develop additional new products.

Sally knew that if she could demonstrate an understanding of such factors as inventory management and finance, it would show she had the knowledge and interest to deal with parts of the business other than marketing. This was a great way to exhibit her ability to not only drive the top line, but control the bottom line as well. The result: she was able to chart a whole new career path.

Leslie is another example. A technical manager in manufacturing operations, she focused on how well products met manufacturing standards and specifications. This was a good but dead-end job, and if she wanted to make more money and move up the organization, she needed a different career path.

She developed competencies in not just how products met specifications, but how the manufacturing process could be modified and improved.

Leslie showed she was not only proficient in understanding technical product specifications like stress levels, capacity utilization, and raw material composition, but also understood some of the broader issues regarding labor costs, distribution efficiencies, economic ordering quantities, and the like. She was curious about the total supply chain, not just her small part of it and she spent time going out with drivers and visiting suppliers to understand the business from their viewpoint. Over time, she was seen as a resource in many areas of the business and she led cross-functional project teams that generated solutions optimal for all functional areas.

All of this effort demonstrated her knowledge in a variety of areas and positioned her as an operations manager. She is now in line to become a vice president of manufacturing.

Suzanne is another successful rebrander. With an Associate of Arts degree, she worked for a music company as an administrative assistant. There, she demonstrated not only an ability to type and manage paper, but much more. Eventually, she was moved into the creative area and positioned herself as the creative assistant to the president of the company. But she didn't stop there. She studied the music industry, and spent time with artists to understand how they produced songs and promoted their craft. She also spent a lot of time learning about music trends and determining why certain sounds were gaining traction among different audience groups. She discovered she had a good ear for what people really like and what appealed to different groups.

But more, she worked hard to understand the production and distribution aspects of the business, and how to get promoters excited about investing in certain music groups. She began to prescreen groups who wanted an audience with senior management and made sure musicians' proposals were structured in a way that addressed all the issues management wanted to know about.

The music groups appreciated this also, because they were able to be more thorough with their presentations, and management appreciated her thoroughness and understanding of the process. After demonstrating her abilities relating to both the music itself and its distribution, she continued to be promoted and now, 20 years later, is president of a major entertainment company that produces movies, plays, and television programs.

Another example is one I read about in *The New York Times,* which published an article about a man laid off from a database marketing company where he was a technical product manager. While searching for work, he helped a company president define a position the president wanted filled. This position was called a product manager, but the man who was looking for work explained to the president that what was needed was not just a marketing professional, but someone who could create a plan that addressed customer needs and the future of the company's product.

This discussion triggered in the man some soul-searching, and he decided he wanted to do what he had described to the president, namely a more customer- and market-focused position, rather than his previous position, which was more operational and technical. Through an acquaintance, he learned of a marketing coordinator job at a company that provides various services for websites. The job sounded too junior for him, but he talked to the CEO and, as he put it: "I told him [the CEO] my ideas, he liked what I had to say and he hired me. I had never talked myself into a role in a company before." Through his creativity and enthusiasm, he rebranded himself from the technical and operational to more marketing and strategic. He was searching for a job for almost a year and was getting disheartened. When he rebranded himself, he was able to get a job in three months!

Karen Fisher also has uniquely branded herself. She was formerly editor of *Cosmopolitan* and *American Home* magazines and now is president of Design Previews, representing some of the world's top designers and architects. Known as the "designer matchmaker" for matching top designers to architects, she also is often called a design psychologist because of her uncanny ability to help clients find their ideal match. This unique ability sets her head and shoulders over others in her field, and positions her to stand out among the pack.

Of course, rebranding doesn't apply only to individuals, but to companies as well. As I mentioned in a previous chapter,

Goodwill has rebranded itself in recent years by bringing in higher-priced merchandise and making its stores look more spiffy and inviting. It has a new image and, as a result, is now attracting a more upscale clientele. Pittsburgh, Pennsylvania, was a steel town until the 1970s. The steel mills went away, and Pittsburgh has since successfully rebranded itself with its highly regarded universities, an Andy Warhol museum, good restaurants, cleaner air, and a vibrant and inviting downtown. Today, someone visiting Pittsburgh would hardly know it once relied heavily on the steel industry for its economic base.

Austin, Texas, has long been Texas's state capitol and home to the University of Texas, but was a second-class citizen to the state's two major metropolitan areas, Dallas-Ft. Worth and Houston. It rebranded itself by becoming a high-tech Mecca (it is the home of Dell Computers and other high-tech companies) and an artsy metropolis, particularly known for its active music scene. Austin is now often listed among the 10 most desirable cities in the country. In a state with big name cities that pride themselves on size, Austin stands tall in the saddle!

I used to live in Montclair, N.J., a New York City suburb, and it too has rebranded itself. Once a generic suburb, today it is known as a magnet for actors, writers, and other creative types. It is child friendly, as well as economically, racially, and politically diverse, and has rebranded itself as one of the more livable cities in the country. Montclair is also a very small city with a lot of character. It is sometimes known as the Upper West Side of the suburbs (the Upper West Side of Manhattan is known for its edgy, creative atmosphere). In an age where big is often positioned as better, it has taken pride in its small size and turned this aspect of itself into a competitive advantage.

Another reason to rebrand yourself is when you leave a position and need to do something else. This situation is most publicly seen with retired presidents. Jimmy Carter, after leaving the White House, aligned himself with Habitat for Humanity, worked on verifying elections around the world, and became a prolific writer. He has since won the Nobel Peace Prize. Bill Clinton started a foundation that addresses global peace and health issues. When presidents leave office, they can be at the end of their working careers unless they rebrand themselves. Carter and Clinton have rebranded themselves so they could have second careers.

You may want to rebrand after retiring. Maurice retired from a technical job where he managed a computer department for a nonprofit organization. He read about people retiring, moving to a place with a warm climate not long after, and dying. Studies show people who get involved and have a positive outlook live longer than those who don't. Maurice wanted to extend his life by getting involved with meaningful activities, but do something different than he did before retiring. He decided to sell African masks, which he learned about from the nonprofit he worked for. He targeted vacation spots like Martha's Vineyard in Massachusetts and the Hamptons in New York as places to sell the masks and to educate people about them. When we last spoke, Maurice had just gotten his business off the ground, and its long-term success was not yet known, but he is optimistic.

Retirement planning is more than a financial plan. You need a social plan of what you will do besides just collecting a check or sitting on the beach. Sitting on the beach is fine as long as it part of your plan and how you want to proceed with your life. A doctor friend reports she has women patients with retired husbands who say they wish their men would do something because they try to run the house now that they are retired. And her retired male patients say they are bored and they and their wives are getting in each other's way. These folks did not plan for how they would live in retirement and what their new roles would be. You have to plan for the back nine holes of your life.

Rebrand to appeal to a different group or market

We talked about Apple, which is my poster child for a company that rebranded itself into the entertainment and communication areas. They have created a consumer base among many who wouldn't have even thought of getting some of these types of computer gadgets before.

Many people do not know that Will Smith, the movie star, began his career not as an actor, but as a music artist. It is surprising how many movie stars started out in different careers. Tracy Marrow, who appears on the television show Law and Order, started as a major singer known as Ice T. He still uses the name Ice T for the most part, but people now don't associate him with singing.

Dana Owens, aka Queen Latifah, underwent rebranding by singing a number of great jazz songs on an album called Traveling Light. People say her voice reminds them of Billie Holiday and Sarah Vaughn. Many Baby Boomers would say so, and they were certainly not part of her original cheering squad.

Often a business wants to appeal to a new market or new consumer base. For years, Brooks Brothers was the gold standard of Madison Avenue and Wall Street, epitomizing conservative business wear. Over the last 10 years, the company has added more flair to its clothing line. Brooks Brothers' embarked on a new direction with a European CEO updating the style of its stores and clothing to appeal to a different market, while still maintaining its old customers. They are rebranding to keep themselves current.

Does everyone have to rebrand?

Does everyone have to rebrand? The answer is emphatically yes. That's because things change and therefore you will have to change. If you don't change, then you are falling behind. It would be fallacious to assume that one can continue the same modus operandi in the future and have it work for you the same way it did years before. As others all around you change, you have to at least determine how you keep up!

Organizations have to change also. Consider some of the tectonic shifts occurring in the population. The so-called minority population of the U.S. is on the path to becoming the majority. By 2050, not that far in the future, the nonwhite population will be the majority. Women now make up more than 50% of the workforce. Organizations have to rebrand to meet the needs of diverse populations, women, younger people, and other groups that are becoming increasingly large and influential. This rebranding will entail changing their recruiting and retention programs to accommodate new employee populations. It will mean that training programs will have to be developed which teach cross-cultural competencies. As the pool of diverse employees increases, organizations will have to demonstrate that they are more inclusive and sensitive to the unique talents and needs of these groups.

As health care improves, people will live longer, which means that organizations that provide products and services catering to this generation will receive attention.

When we consider the changes that have occurred in the last 10 to 20 years, we can easily witness the adjustments that organizations have already made to stay relevant. For example, the Internet has created a sea change in terms of how we get information and communicate with each other. This means that if organizations want to reach consumers differently, they need to develop the internal capabilities to expand their reach. It is now commonplace to see business cards with a phone number, work address, email address and website. This was not the case even 15 years ago.

Being better than you believe means rethinking your current business model. Consumer tastes will continue to demand new services and products. As consumers continue to want more convenience, variety, and efficiency in their products and services, organizations will have to keep up with their requirements. To retain your consumers and ensure brand loyalty, you must satisfy your customers' needs.

As businesses become increasingly global, they must consider how they will rebrand to appeal to different populations in other countries. Many fast food chains that originated in the U.S. are still seen as very Western oriented and not catering to local consumer tastes. In order to adjust to local consumer preferences, they should adopt some of the flavors, scents and smells that can increase local appeal. Disney with its theme park in Paris provides a good example of the challenge in this area. Disney has changed its image and rebranded itself to be more acceptable to the local population. It changed its menu by adopting more local food and built more outdoor seating at its restaurants to accommodate the European preference for outdoor dining. It also changed the name of its French park from Euro-Disney to Disneyland Paris, and incorporated more local cultural flavor. The result is that Disneyland Paris has more attendance than the Louvre and Eiffel Tower combined. It is important for global companies to reflect the local culture and cater to local needs. Even though many countries desire certain U.S. food establishments, they may want to see some aspect of their local culture on the menu. For example, a major U.S. coffee chain adopted some of the local themes in its beverage and pastry section in England. This is what being global and thinking local is all about.

Every person and every organizational entity needs to review the direction in which it is proceeding. Usually organizations start the beginning of the year with a new budget, but they don't take the time to decide whether they are going to achieve the budget with the same set of assumptions as before. They may even put a lot of effort into determining how the market is changing, but not put as much time into deciding how they need to adjust to capture new market share.

Unfortunately, many small businesses that need to rebrand the most are the entities that do it the least. Often Fortune 500 companies have built-in organizational mechanisms that force a periodic review of their present positioning. They have boards of directors, marketing departments, long range planning professionals, and marketing research capabilities that engage in periodic reviews that involve examining their brand.

Many entrepreneurs don't engage in this evaluation and suffer as a result. Socrates said that an unexamined life is not worth living. I would say that an individual or organization that doesn't engage in a serious reexamination of itself every year is failing to capitalize on how it can improve and reach new heights.

How do you rebrand?

Whether you have been presented with a new opportunity, feel you are at a dead end, or you are transitioning from one point to another, you may need to start with a new vision of yourself. Re-examining your vision, reviewing your values, and revisiting your distinctive competencies are all part of the re-branding process. Do a hard assessment of your current brand to decide if it is right for you, or if you should move in a different direction.

At this point, you are at the fork in the road I call the decision point. At the decision point you begin to ask the question: Who do I want to be? What you decide to do based on this feedback determines whether you continue with your present brand or rebrand and set off in a new direction. This is the difficult part because many organizations and individuals just stop at this point. They don't begin the step of self-determination that rebrands them. The process of rebranding is a creative act, and it renews and invigorates. Rebranding allows you to take advantage of new opportunities, directions, markets, and customers. You can now ensure your concept is aligned with the new vision you have outlined, and that your distinctive competencies enable you to shine over others. Rebranding cannot take place unless you look at it within the context of your vision, values, and distinctive competencies.

It is difficult to do this alone. Everyone needs help, so you need to engage others to help you with the rebranding process, which is the subject of the next chapter

Thought Stimulators

Ask yourself:

1. What is your personal brand?

Now that you have identified your vision, values, and competencies, it will be much easier to identify a personal brand that incorporates each of these elements. When developing your personal brand, address all three of these areas. Make your description specific.

2. Is your personal brand aligned with your vision?

Clarify that the brand you have identified for yourself is the brand you want to have, or if you want something else. If your "brand" is someone who is efficient, is that the "brand" you want going forward? You may want to expand it by saying you want to be efficient and effective with resources, and to be ecologically minded and socially responsible in a way that facilitates financial well being. This is more all encompassing and takes into account a different vision for your role in the world and your relationship with significant others.

3. Based on your vision, values, and distinctive competencies, how would you rebrand yourself to be more effective and satisfied?

Answer this question in the future tense: I am now...

Examples: If a person does not own his or her own house but wants to: I am now a homeowner. If a person wants to be married: I am now married. Or I now have my own boutique store selling sports clothes in Denver, Colorado.

4. *What is the present brand of your business or organization? How would you rebrand it to be more relevant, productive, effective, and stronger?*

Let's say your organization has a very strong domestic based U.S. brand that is present in all 50 states. You may want to rebrand in order to establish a global presence in emerging markets in BRIC countries. Alternatively, you may want to move the HQ of your organization to Dubai from Singapore or the UK.

Describe your new brand in the future tense. For example, we are now the primary distributor of olive oil in Canada. Our firm is now among the top three producers of widgets in the Dominican Republic.

Chapter 7
Your Personal Board of Directors

It is not the strongest of the species that survives, or the most intelligent, but the ones most responsive to change.

Charles Darwin

Intelligence and strength are not enough to survive

Let's face it, many of us feel that some people succeed because they are smart or strong or good looking or have the right family connections or were born in the right ZIP Code. The fact is, while these factors might work to some extent, rarely are they enough. Personal success is seldom the result of the efforts of the individual alone. Most of us need to involve others in order to succeed.

One of the greatest thinkers in recorded history, Isaac Newton, famously said, "If I have seen a little further, it is by standing on the shoulders of giants." He was referring to his ability to see -- to understand -- science a bit better than others because of the work done by his predecessors.

BEING BETTER THAN YOU BELIEVE

If Newton was willing to admit he had to rely on others for his success, in this case scientists who came before him, you too should consider your need to rely on others for your success. We are all interconnected in this world. In organizations, we connect with significant others to implement our plans. Our families and community groups enable us to fulfill our basic needs and relate to others.

It is true that no man or woman is an island. Whether we are part of a social club, religious institution, or corporation, we all interface with others. However, we do not always go the next step to really cultivate relationships that are in sync with our vision and goals. Often our relationships are very superficial. It is important to take the time to deepen certain relationships that can facilitate our goals. We don't get the full potential that certain relationships offer because we don't go beyond cursory and casual interactions. By being more strategic and purposeful, we can really get the full potential out of our relationships. This is what networking is about.

Getting a job is an example. The United States Bureau of Labor Statistics reports that 70% of individuals find their jobs through networking. Networking is another word for relying on others. Think of your network as your *personal board of directors.* Understanding what networking is, how to do it effectively, and how to use it to achieve your vision is critical to your success.

What networking is not

Usually people think networking is only about getting a job or making a connection at a social event where they trade business cards, but networking is much more. Here is my definition of networking: Developing and maintaining quality and mutually beneficial relationships and making this process a way of life. Probably the most important aspect of this definition regards maintaining quality relationships. Often people are good at developing relationships, but they don't do enough to maintain them and sustain the efficacy that derives from establishing the relations in the first place. I will address this in more detail later.

Some people seem to have networking built into their DNA; they appear to do it naturally. But actually that is more myth than reality. Networking is an acquired set of behaviors and skills related to developing relationships. These you can learn, just as you learn how to play golf or become an effective public speaker. And the payoff for mastering networking is significant. When you develop relationships, you gain accessibility: accessibility to information, resources, contacts, influence, and insights.

Another networking myth is that you need it only when you want to find or change jobs. It has value far beyond job seeking, which is why you must always do it. Networking creates a number of benefits, such as learning about aspects of your work from someone you network with, and using these insights to make you more effective at your job. Bottom line:

Even when not looking for employment, networking brings benefits.

Further, people think being friendly and meeting people in high places is networking. Being friendly is part of networking and is necessary, but it is not enough. It certainly is good to be seen as approachable so that people want to get to know you better. What is commonly mistaken for being friendly is when you have a disposition that invites others to continue associating with you. You may be approachable and don't offend them. You make others feel comfortable confiding in you or revealing their most innermost thoughts. You may be a good listener.

Let me point out that good listening is a skill, and though good listening is not sufficient to make someone a good networker, it is necessary for networking. Many have trouble listening; yet listening, like networking, is something which can be learned. A good listener acknowledges what people have said and clarifies points to make sure the listener understands. They pause from interrupting others and let the other person get their full thoughts out. They say words which encourage the other to say more. Sometimes it is just an affirmative nod or a small statement like, "tell me more about that." Speakers appreciate this because they want to be understood correctly. In a world where superficiality sometimes reigns, authentic and sincere discourse that enlightens, informs, and entertains is refreshing. Listening is part of good networking, but not all of it.

Additionally, some believe if they network with the appropriate person, this individual will become a mentor and help them reach most of their personal goals. All they need is this one person. Well, one person cannot do that. Almost everyone needs a group of people to rely on. This group I call your *personal board of directors*.

Your Personal Board of Directors

Organizations have boards of directors who give guidance, advice and oversight in very specific areas to the CEO and senior management team. The CEO benefits greatly because he or she uses this input to guide the organization. Why should the CEO have all the fun? Every person can develop his or her own *Personal Board of Directors* or PBOD. This concept is one way to organize those who would help you achieve your goals.

The PBOD is a virtual group. They don't meet with each other, and they may not even know each other, but they all serve a purpose. Basically, a board consists of people who have very distinct contributions and skills. The most beneficial boards have a diversity of abilities and perspectives.

The benefit of the PBOD is that you can essentially have a number of people in your network who each offer different perspectives. When you think about your network, consider your goals and who can help you achieve them. Some individuals look for one or two mentors who can meet most of their needs; however, this is not practical or recommended. You want to expand your repertoire of advisers by thinking about what your needs or goals are first, and then who can help you with these goals. There are a number of goals that most people have in mind when networking, but let us consider the major goals that serve as beneficial reasons to network.

Four benefits of networking

As I see it, networking provides four major benefits:

1. Access to people

Building strong relationships with others in and out of your organization provides access to people to whom you normally do not have access. People in different departments and different companies can provide information useful in your job, of course, but also information about job opportunities, social or recreational opportunities, trends in your industry, and much more.

Networking gives you accessibility you would not normally have. We network to gain access to people who can help us. Because many of us are deeply mired in the details of our jobs, we don't often make the time to go outside our usual circle of acquaintances. This limits our perspective, our information, and our ability to get things done. It is amazing what doors will open when we get additional insight and perspective we would not normally receive. When we just rely on a small circle of friends, we limit our ability to really access others who can give us assistance.

A colleague, Hassan, born overseas, moved to the U.S. where he earned a Ph.d in engineering and was highly respected in the research center where he worked. He was somewhat isolated; he knew the people in his department, but few outside it. He lacked the insight or connections to move his career to the next level. We talked about how he could meet other people outside his small circle of friends, and targeted three people he should get to know better and who could offer him advice on how to progress in the organization.

Each of these individuals had a unique perspective. One worked overseas, and provided an outsider's view on Hassan's employer (being an employee often makes it difficult to have an unbiased view of one's employer). Another personal board member was new to the company but had worked at several other companies, was very experienced, and was able to provide Hassan with guidance on how to work one's way up a corporate ladder. The third person was an executive who had a similar career track as Hassan and who could talk about what he did to get ahead. Often it is very difficult to get effective advice from those in your organization, because you are competing against them. This particular person had already gotten ahead and took pride in mentoring others and helping them get ahead.

What Hassan gained from this PBOD was how to work more effectively from a cross-cultural standpoint, how to understand the corporate environment, how to improve his

English-language skills and how to understand the similarities and differences compared with the country where he was born.

2. *Access to resources*

Ultimately, we want access to people because they can provide information, resources, influence and insight. Networking is not primarily for socializing. We are looking for people who can give us the wherewithal to influence those things that are important to us. We network because we want to get assistance in meeting critical goals. We network to get perspective that we don't presently have.

These goals may be professional or personal, but certainly we cannot accomplish them without having added insight from others. Quite frankly, your boss or significant other can help you only to a certain extent. Beyond that, you need others involved to execute your plans and provide additional perspective.

Let me give you another example. Juan wanted to understand how to influence a bill in the legislature that would affect his ability to import spare parts from the Caribbean, which was his business. He needed to know whom to contact when critical legislation was being discussed in committee before it came to the floor for a full Senate vote, so he attended a number of social events and fundraisers, but didn't seem to connect to the right people. Connecting him to a retired legislator who really knew how things worked would be critical in this situation. This individual had no vested interest or expectation of financial gain and was very willing to help Juan. Hence, he was a great resource for Juan's *personal board of directors*.

3. Networking helps you get results quicker

To execute your business goals and objectives requires access to certain information and resources. You might want information on what competitors are doing or what is happening in the economy quicker than you can get it from the media or even the internet. Networking can get you such information before it hits the public domain. The speed of response will make you more effective than others who are not getting that information as quickly, providing you with a competitive advantage.

Lobbyists spend millions of dollars getting access to new policies or legislation that are being developed in local, state, and federal governments. For a company to understand what laws may be enacted that will affect their business is extremely important. Getting information quickly by networking enables you to respond quicker than those who don't have this information. Again, networking is about relationships, and relationships are about accessibility.

Sometimes your need is very short-term and you just need to understand how to facilitate your work. Barbara was very well connected as a reporter, but needed information regarding the effect of budget cuts on staffing patterns in a school and she needed it quickly to meet her deadline. She avoided the Mayor's office because she thought they would give her the company line and refer her to the chief public relations officer. However, one of her ex-professors from college, with whom she had remained in contact, happened to be working in that office and said if she came to a lunchtime conference and met with the chief public relations officer on an informal basis, she would get more candid information. This person was immensely helpful in providing her with the perspective she needed.

4. *Letting others know who you are and what you can do*

It is not uncommon for someone to think technical competence is sufficient to be recognized and promoted. In fact, technical competence is almost never enough to get the attention of others. You also must market yourself by communicating to significant others the benefits you can provide the organization. These significant others might be stakeholders in your company or stakeholders in your professional circle, such as your trade or professional organization.

Sometimes we wonder why certain people appear on television or are quoted in publications, when we feel we have more knowledge. Often, the missing ingredient is networking. Some people are well networked, while others are not. Those well networked make themselves known to the media, and get media exposure even when others are more knowledgeable. Those seen on television or quoted in newspapers, websites, or blogs know how to market themselves via networking.

Roberto needed to understand how to market his capabilities more effectively. He had an excellent reputation as a professor of Ecological and Environmental Studies, but he needed to develop a national reputation in his field if he was going to reach his goal of becoming the chairman of the department. Of course, he published many articles, which is important in academia, and this worked out well, but he needed to do more if he would reach his goal of being department chair.

After some coaching, he joined professional associations to get insights and contacts. When he joined a group that was on the cutting edge of the conservation movement, he aligned with another professor who took him under his wing. Roberto did joint presentations at conferences with this professor, who also got Roberto involved in several committees so he could become better known. These activities helped him be seen in a very different light by his college president and his peers, and he was invited to coordinate a number of symposiums at his college. While he has not been promoted to department head yet, he certainly has more visibility and this will definitely help him reach his goal. In private conversations, I ascertained that he was on the short list of candidates to be considered for department chair, which was not the case before.

Why don't we network more often?

Many feel networking is all about currying favor with the expectation of getting something in return, and so they are reluctant to do it. Networking can involve currying favor, but that is a very short-term view. Effective networking requires you develop long-term meaningful relationships.

For others, networking may not come naturally. Introverts, for instance, may struggle to network because it works against their natural tendencies. As I mentioned above, networking is a learned skill, so even if it does not come naturally, you can master it.

Fear of rejection plays a big part of why some do not network. Approaching a stranger or a high-level executive creates anxiety about being rejected. This fear of rejection is a powerful deterrent and limits one's ability to reach out in different ways.

To overcome this fear, ask yourself, "What is the worst that can happen?" Our fear of what will occur is usually worse than what might actually occur. Of course, fear often stems from lack of confidence in these situations. As you network, you will likely find people are more willing to share information and help you than you originally thought.

When you have not done something before, fear sets in because of the unknown. Once you try it the first time, your confidence increases. It is like swimming in the ocean. You may be afraid the water will be cold, but once you get in, you acclimate to the water and feel fine. Ultimately, fear is overcome with confidence gained from experience. When you think of the pay-off of stretching beyond your present psychological boundaries, then you can begin to see the benefits of taking risks.

Time is a scarce resource for us all, and we often feel we do not have time to network. We view networking as a luxury we cannot afford. We set priorities and networking is just not high on our list. Keith Ferrazzi, in his book, "Never Eat Alone," highlights how important it is to use your time differently to build productive relationships. Some people lunch alone at their desk. Lunchtime, says Ferrazzi, is better spent networking. Some people eat with the same people every day and do not venture outside their department or professional group. In fact, many company cafeterias might as well have name plaques on some seats because certain people sit in the same place, week after week, year after year.

Even if you eat with someone different just twice a week, you can make significant progress toward your networking goal. Go to work a little earlier and have coffee or tea with someone you have wanted to connect with. There is always time. It is a matter of choices, which is why you must take stock of the time you waste and determine how to turn it into productive time. Instead of going home every day after work, consider attending a professional forum or organization membership meeting. Again, it is all a matter of choices.

Finally, we all have a tendency to interact with those we know. Many of us spend almost all of our time with those we already know and have known for many years, rather than stretching and meeting new people. Some of this is cultural, as we feel a greater affinity and more comfort talking to those who share our ethnic, national, religious, economic, or other background. We don't cross over and talk to others outside of these "boundaries."

To break out of this regimen, understand you can learn from others outside of your"world" by developing an appreciation for others who are different from you and have different perspectives from your own. "If everybody thinks the same, then nobody is thinking," is what Einstein said.

Your *personal board of directors* should consist of those who can give you different perspectives. If you just connect with the "amen corner" -- people who will just affirm what you already know -- then you aren't getting the critical input that can stretch you and help you improve.

What can you do to overcome your networking barriers?

View networking as a necessity

First, recognize networking as a necessity. When we talk about necessities, we think about food, clothing, and shelter. Many do not feel they need networking, let alone think of it as a necessity. But once you identify your vision and how you want to achieve your personal goals, you will find you can't do it alone, which is why you need to network.

Demonstrate an interest in others

Some of us are so centered on ourselves that we are not able to demonstrate an interest in others. Demonstrating an interest in other people is essential, and networking can help you achieve this. It shows you care about others, are curious about them, and have a real interest in their success. This will be of enormous help with your own success.

Networking is not a one-way street. By demonstrating an interest in others, you also begin to show an interest in mentoring others. Giving to others insights and assistance is as valuable to you as to the receiver. Unselfishness pays off because what you give will come back to you tenfold.

A friend, who is 75 years old, says that during her working life, she always had a mentor who was older than she and another who was younger. Hence, her PBOD had someone who had the wisdom of age to point out what might be tried and true, and a younger vision to keep her fresh and vital with new insights and ways of looking at the world.

Her approach really diversified her PBOD. The problem with many boards is they lack diversity and fail to provide fresh perspectives and rich insights.

Maintaining your network

When you think of networking, it is not enough to build your network. Even more important is maintaining it as I stated earlier. Many people start a network but don't maintain it, so the benefits from it remain unrealized. To maintain your network:

1. Don't wait for a crisis before you begin to network

I am constantly approached by individuals who haven't contacted me in a year or more, who say, "Remember me? Can you help me find a job?" Or, "Will you give me a reference?" In many cases I will do it, but the point is, stay connected and do not just wait for a pressing need to get in touch with your network.

Networks like other things in life require constant maintenance. You don't wait for your car to breakdown before you change the oil. You don't wait for a toothache to happen to get your teeth checked and cleaned. You don't wait for a heart attack to get an annual physical exam.

Don't wait until you are in desperate need before you contact people in your network. Keep in contact with everyone in your network at least twice a year. In fact, have a PBOD gathering so you can benefit from the synergies of having all of your advisors cross-fertilizing ideas and perspectives. The goal: building the foundation for the networking relationship.

2. Keep in touch by remembering special events

Meetings and lunches are not necessary to maintain contact with your network. Congratulate those in your network for certain events -- the anniversary of you both starting a job or starting college, a marriage in their family, their birthday or wedding anniversary, the birth of a child. This goes a long way toward maintaining contact and keeping your network strong and effective. It adds the personal touch that is so vital to keeping a relationship strong. Your goal: keep the connection active.

3. Ask for advice or input on just about anything

Most people who know about a topic are very willing to give you advice. If you took an economics class with someone, ask what they think next year's economy will look like. The advice doesn't have to be profound. You just might want to know about an opera or jazz performance. Do they know a great Thai or French restaurant? The goal: keep people thinking about you; stay "top of mind."

4. Contact at special intervals

There are always intervals in one's life when it makes sense to talk to someone. At the beginning of the summer, ask what they plan to do during the summer. At the end of the summer, ask how their summer was. Such communication maintains the connection and provides interesting information about how a person's life is going and evolving. The goal: letting them know you are in their thoughts.

5. Let's do lunch

This is a phrase used when someone sees a person they have not seen in a long time, but the promise to do lunch often lacks serious commitment. Make it a commitment! Follow up when you run into someone. Do lunch, or have coffee or tea during the workday or a drink after work. Such brief connections go a long way toward maintaining your networking and keeping you "top-of-mind "with that individual. The goal: showing a sincere desire to keep the network strong and ongoing.

How to build your network

When starting to build your network, first consider your personal and professional goals, because with these identified, it is much easier to identify those who will facilitate your achieving those goals. This is where your PBOD comes in.

Let's say you have a goal to move to a new city. You will want to network with those who can advise you on the cost of living in the city, the schools, the public transit options, the benefits of the city, the characteristics of various neighborhoods, where your spouse might get a job, and the like. Maybe you could get all this from one person, but probably you will need to connect with two or three or four individuals. They become members of your *personal board of directors*, a group that will assist you to meet your goal of moving to the city.

Working your six degrees of separation

It is often said that we are no more than *six degrees of separation* from you and everyone else in the world. Whether the real number is six or something else, it is important to realize that connecting with one individual provides connections to many other individuals.

As I have gone through life, I am probably no more than three degrees separated from a number of people. I have never met Nobel Peace Prize winner Nelson Mandela of South Africa, but I am not far separated from him. I once moderated a seminar in South Africa with someone who worked for a sister of a famous South African singer. This singer was once in Mandela's cabinet. So I am only a few degrees separated from Mandela, if I wanted to try to connect with him in order to reach my personal goals. Don't get me wrong. I have no plans to try to reach out to Nelson Mandela, but am using this as an illustration of how a network of people, a PBOD, can provide potential access to many people.

Technology through social networking sites such as LinkedIn and Facebook can facilitate your networking efforts. Though such technology is not as personal as talking to someone in person, it could help you expand and maintain your network. Unfortunately, some people just collect names and elaborate about how many people are on their LinkedIn and Facebook sites. A network needs to be maintained and nourished. It is better to have fewer people on your electronic network whom you really cultivate than to have thousands whom you will have nothing to do with after they have signed on.

Another way to connect with people is by expanding the *"connect points"* you have with individuals. A connect point is a link to something you have in common with a person. The more you have in common, the stronger the connection and relationship.

Recently I met Vanessa, a college student. At first we just connected in the area of education; she is a student at a local college. She attended a conference at the school where I was the keynote speaker. As I talked with her, I learned she lived right near the block where I grew up in Brooklyn. Also, she had relatives in a section of the Caribbean I have visited many times and, it turned out, we knew individuals there in common. Furthermore, she had an interest in music and art, and I learned she frequents a music venue where I also have Board affiliation. From a simple *connect point* relating to education, I quickly found we had several other *connect points* that could be valuable if we choose to stay connected.

Your potential points of entry with others are wide ranging, from sports to travel, hobbies, schooling, where you live (or where you are going to live), food, occupation, and others. When you begin to explore many of these *connect points,* you deepen and broaden the relationship you have with others. Sometimes these connections start very casually and then deepen as you continually explore your points of commonality.

When speaking at a conference in Los Angeles, I met a

soft drink distributor who had a new product. It just so happens that in New York I have a relationship with a company promoting this product, so I used this connect point to deepen my relationship with this distributor and hope this will result in my being a keynote speaker at one of the distributor's sales conventions. You never know where your network will take you.

Networking can be the foundation that will create new opportunities you wouldn't have believed possible. Chapter 8 will tell you how to create opportunities for your continued success.

Thought Stimulators

Ask yourself:

1.   Identify your present mentors and list what they offer.

Think in terms of the goals for networking which includes information, resources, access, insight, and influence.

2.   Identify specific gaps that exist in terms of your networking goals.

Examples: Are there specific resources you need but don't have? Is there access you need that doesn't presently exist? Be specific.

3. *Identify two people who can be potential mentors to you in the areas where you have gaps.*

If you can't think of a specific person, then identify who might introduce you and connect you to a person who can help you meet your goals.

4. *For the mentors you presently have, identify the three strongest connect points.*

A *connect point* is a focus area you have in common with an individual. If you meet an individual on the job, your connect point is work. But this relationship is strengthened if you live in the same neighborhood, which allows you to connect in terms of transportation, recreational activities, or even restaurants or entertainment. Maybe you have vacationed in the same place or like certain recreational activities like skiing, swimming, or mountain climbing. Perhaps you both like action movies or museums. These are areas where you can find something in common with your mentor. Connect points strengthen relationships.

5. *Identify at least two more connect points for each of the mentors you have on your personal board of directors.*

Chapter 8
Creating Opportunities for Success

When life hands you lemons, make lemonade.

Anonymous

When I was 15 years old, I had a paper route in an inner city neighborhood of Brooklyn, New York. Each night I picked up a stack of three different local newspapers at a nearby newsstand, and went to certain neighborhoods, stores, and bars to sell them. I would start with five copies of each paper, priced at 5 cents apiece, and when these were sold, I would return to the newsstand, buy more, and return to the places where I sold. My route wasn't a designated one like newspaper boys had in the suburbs. It was a route I created myself. I would just walk through neighborhoods for two to three hours where there were no newspaper stands or other places that sold newspapers, and sell my papers to the people there who lacked convenient access to newspapers.

I sold newspapers after school and on weekends because I

needed money. My parents could not afford to give me an allowance. There were few jobs in my neighborhood and none for someone my age. Selling newspapers was how I earned money. Out of necessity, I have often taken an opportunity where there didn't seem to be any, and turned it into success.

From this and other experiences, several elements come to mind that helped me turn opportunity into success.

Optimism

It is important to have a positive perspective about situations. Even when facing adversity, you need to believe you can succeed. This perspective can lead to even more opportunities, which will lead to more successes. Viewing situations positively rather than negatively has an exponential effect. It determines your approach and how you will take advantage of situations. If you are able to successfully take advantage of situations that seem insurmountable, you have turned them to your advantage.

This often applies in adversarial situations, whether war, business, or one's personal life. Our perspective helps ensure that negative situations are not insurmountable. Essentially, any situation can be viewed in two ways, namely positively (in an optimistic fashion) or negatively (in a pessimistic fashion).

Pessimism breeds inaction and passivity. When you are thinking things will not work out well, you tend to sit around waiting for things to happen. When optimistic, you have a can-do attitude and are energized because you believe you can overcome obstacles and succeed. Rather than waiting around for something to happen, try a variety of approaches and keep trying until you get what you want. Be determined because you believe you can succeed which, in turn, increases your chances to succeed.

Often, whether you succeed or fail is only a matter of perspective. Few who doubt their ability to succeed have, in fact, become shining successes. The history of entrepreneurship is filled with stories of people who believe they would succeed while surrounded by others who were convinced they would fail.

I have talked about steps to build your confidence -- understanding yourself, understanding others, having a goal or vision, and having a plan. All of these help to build your optimism because now you are aware of the enabling factors that assist you to overcome the walls that previously seemed insurmountable.

Creating Opportunities for Success

Keep an open mind

Keeping an open mind and having a positive outlook are essential. A positive outlook opens you to taking advantage of situations. Don't have a narrow focus, and keep your options open. This provides flexibility when you approach situations.

People with a narrow outlook become fixated on one way to do things, which is a formula for disaster. An open mind makes you receptive to many options that can open opportunities for you in ways you normally would not have seen.

Do your homework and know your stuff

When confronted with any situation, really know your material. Sometimes your understanding of what to do may not be clear, and you have to work to understand the situation. Do not expect it all to be easy. The best way take advantage of any opportunities that might arise is to be really prepared. It's the 5 "P" theory: Proper Planning Prevents Poor Performance!

There is a connection between hard work and success. Thomas Edison made the observation: "Opportunity is missed by most people because it is dressed up in overalls and looks like work."

Taking advantage of opportunities does require effort. It is not an easy road, but a road that will bring benefits if you are willing to pay the price. The price is blood, sweat and tears. In other words, there will be many difficult challenges to overcome but the likely outcome makes it all worthwhile. Many people want the benefits, but will not always do what is necessary to get those benefits. The results will speak for themselves once you make the effort.

Position yourself for the long term

The best way to create opportunities for success is to position yourself for the long term. Looking for short-term success should not be the goal. A focus on short-term success will likely make you miss the really important long-term opportunities that come your way.

That does not mean you should ignore small opportunities. These very often lead to major successes. I have a friend, who is a management consultant, who wanted to win a major contract with a manufacturing based firm. She was asked to take on a training opportunity of a small department in the warehouse area that initially didn't seem worth the trouble. The good news is that she received such excellent ratings that they asked her to train several other departments and the next year she was hired on retainer to conduct a series of workshops over a two year period.

Small opportunities can lead to major successes if you take a long-term view.

I've heard Oprah Winfrey say: "Luck is preparation meeting opportunity." You need to be prepared. You cannot count on luck to make you successful.

Have faith in yourself

You need faith in yourself. One of the movies I enjoy is the classic, "The Wizard of Oz." The story behind the three characters who accompany Dorothy along the Yellow Brick

Road is this: The Tin Man did not know he had sensitivity; the Scarecrow did not know he had intelligence; and the Lion did not know he had courage. Of course, they all had what they thought they lacked.

I have a good friend who often identifies with the lion, who didn't at first feel he had the courage needed to be successful. Take a moment to consider situations where you found yourself overwhelmed and how you reacted. This will help you gain insights into your strengths and gain faith in your abilities. Likely, you will find you have a lot more character, fortitude, substance, and capability than you originally thought.

Where is the puck going?

Wayne Gretzky was perhaps the greatest hockey player of all time. He stated that a good hockey player goes to where the puck will be, not where it is. It is so important to have foresight and be future oriented, and to think a few steps ahead about any situation you happen to be in. If you like to play chess, as I do, you know you cannot be successful just thinking about your next move. You have to think several moves ahead. If you are able to think a few moves ahead in life, dealing with difficult situations will be easier.

- When we look at the present global situation and all of the crises facing us, where is the puck going?

- Where will the puck be going with regard to the

healthcare needs of people not only in the U.S., but around the world?

• Can we think ahead about trends in the area of education when we find that in many countries, the reading and mathematical levels of a large portion of the populace are not up to standards?

• What will the future hold when we realize there are going to be issues with energy and diminishing supplies of natural resources?

• What are the implications as citizens to handle these global issues and also as individuals coming into the world of work? Individuals graduating from school and looking for jobs need to think about what their occupation will be. When we can visualize what the future may hold for us, we can begin to prepare for those future scenarios. That preparation may entail learning new skills and carving roads in uncharted waters.

Those who have foresight can begin to see what role they will play in these future scenarios. We may need a body of knowledge to do it. We may need people available who can develop solutions. We may need people with the knowledge, skill, and resources to handle many different crises and situations. We have to look forward to see what we need to put in place to be successful. Opportunities arise when you have individuals with the foresight to see the trends that are taking place and know how to take advantage of them.

When you have the ability to visualize future trends, you can determine how you fit in the picture. The Kauffman Foundation conducted a study called, " The Economic Future Just Happened," that found over half the companies on the 2009 list of the Fortune 500 and almost half of the firms on the 2008 list of America's Fastest Growing Companies were founded during an economic recession or bear market! Some of these are today icons of success: FedEx, Hyatt, CNN, MTV, Burger King, and *Sports Illustrated*. Why is this important? Some would say that a recession is the worst time to start a new business. These companies did the unthinkable and they are now very successful. They went against the tide and created their own opportunities.

Turning obstacles into opportunity is a creative act

All of the problems and obstacles that seem in place are really opportunities, if people see their potential. Alexander Graham Bell said, "People sometimes stare so long at the door that is closing that they miss the one which is opening." When one door closes, often another opens, if we are open to this new opportunity.

Many of us spend so much time worrying about what is needed that we don't look at what is there that can be used to turn situations around. Certainly, turning situations around by using a different perspective is a lonely road. In his noted book "Walden," Henry David Thoreau said, "We may sometimes march to the beat of a different drummer." This is fine, but when doing this, we must be *better than we believe.*

Success requires charting new paths and directions, breaking from the pack, and setting up a vision that may not have been in place before. The benefit is a payoff that is rich, sustaining, and fulfilling in every way.

Fight self-defeating behaviors

It's not always easy to turn obstacles into opportunities. Unfortunately, we may have behaviors that hold us back and inhibit our ability to take advantage of opportunities that are right in front of us.

The first step is to understand our behaviors and determine to what extent these behaviors are facilitating or inhibiting our ability to get what we want. This self-awareness is critical if we are to move forward. It is incredible how many barriers we create for ourselves. For example, often we don't share what is happening to us nor communicate our present situation to significant others. Sometimes we are ashamed or embarrassed. Selfish pride gets in the way and prevents us from asking for the help we need.

If you don't share what is happening, then there is no way that others can help you and offer advice. Overcoming this selfish pride can go a long way to getting others enrolled in helping you. Whether it's about getting a job or changing a relationship or dealing with a financial crisis, you can't create an opportunity to change unless you realize that you cannot do it alone. Again, you gain a lot by sharing and involving others. You are not alone, and you may be surprised to find that telling others about your situation is not as difficult or embarrassing as you thought.

Another classic self-defeating behavior is being indecisive. This is the root of procrastination, which is the classic situation of putting something off for tomorrow what should be done today. The irony is that when you are indecisive, you are making a decision to remain in the status quo. You are always making a decision. There is no such thing as a non-decision. Unfortunately the notion of putting off a decision means you are continuing with the present course of action and therefore subject to the consequences of that course of action. Putting off a decision is never a good strategy. It's self-defeating, because it results in a stalemate.

Using networking to create opportunities for success

Earlier we talked about how useful networking is as a mechanism to reach your goals. Networking productively can be a powerful vehicle to create opportunities for success. For example, I renewed a personal contact with a colleague who moved back to the Caribbean from the U.S. after living abroad for almost 20 years.

In the Caribbean, he joined the Rotary Club, local civic associations, and the local church. Not only did he join, but he took on leadership positions on committees. He didn't try to be head of the organizations. He just wanted to join and take on responsible committee assignments that seemed to be neglected and used these to make meaningful contributions to the success of the island.

After a while, he was trusted as someone who would follow through on commitments and could be relied on to help those who needed assistance. His goal was to get reconnected to his home country and make meaningful contributions to the community in his retirement. Within a short period of time he developed a strong reputation for being consistent, dependable, and trustworthy. That is his "personal brand." He now has a whole new career with unexpected benefits.

How involvement in organizations and associations creates opportunities

It is amazing how many people neglect organizations and associations as viable vehicles for networking. For example, colleges and even high schools have alumni associations that are viable for networking. Sure, you can use various alumni social media sites, but what I am referring to is getting involved and reconnecting with past acquaintances in very different ways.

You may find that individuals are in jobs or live in a certain region of the country or the world that may have significance for you. Getting involved in committees and taking on leadership roles enable you to demonstrate your capabilities. Furthermore, it may be that when you were in school people had one view of you, but you have since changed and/or developed in new areas.

Getting involved allows people to rebrand themselves and provide others with a different perspective of themselves.

You can get similar results by getting involved in your professional associations or social clubs. There is not an organization in the world that can't use more arms and legs to accomplish their goals. The same can be said for various employee network groups inside corporations. There is always an opportunity to take the initiative and provide leadership in a way that contributes to the success of the organization. It may be leading a committee assignment, or developing a task force.

When you get involved, that is a good time to see what else needs to be accomplished. It's an opportunity to provide new insights and perspectives. By doing so you also are able to practice new skills and demonstrate your capability in different ways.

For example, Renee was a very good scientist, but her job didn't allow her to exhibit the project management skills she needed to progress in the company. She took on a leadership role with a professional chemists' association as chair of the membership committee and also chaired the cultural committee for her employee network group. These activities not only enabled her to practice project management skills, but also gave her more visibility within her profession. As a result, her superior put her on a temporary assignment to develop new ingredients for a product that would be more economical and environmentally friendly. She demonstrated she could pull together groups of people from different departments, set the project critical path, communicate effectively and work through conflict in a very positive manner. After a year, she was promoted.

Renee was able to use these organizations and associations to demonstrate skills that she didn't have the opportunity to do in her job. As individuals seek to move up the ladder, they find that they need to exhibit other leadership competencies. Technical prowess and knowledge may not be enough to move them forward. They have to show initiative, communication ability, presentation skills, project management ability, and team building capability. They are stymied in their progress because their present job may not offer them opportunities to demonstrate these abilities. That is why involvement in these outside groups can be very beneficial.

Furthermore, as you network in these organizations you also find out about other opportunities you didn't know existed. It was a common adage many years ago that people would find their job in the local newspapers. This is certainly not the case anymore. In fact, with the advent of the web, companies find that 30% or more of job applicants come to them through the Internet. Finding out about how to position yourself for these opportunities comes from networking.

When you are able to put your strategy together and reap the results that accrue, then you are ready to bask in the glow. We will talk about this next.

Thought Stimulators

Ask yourself:

1. Identify two situations in your life where you were able to turn an opportunity into success.

Usually the best indicator of your future success is to identify what made you successful in the past, such as involvement in a situation that really emphasized your values and your capabilities. In the future, you want to call upon the same strength that helped you before. Sometimes we are so caught up in the problems we have in the present that we don't think about how we were able to overcome issues like this in the past. Instead, we focus on our weaknesses and development needs, and do not think about the strengths we have.

2. Describe what you did that enabled you to be successful. Be specific.

Example: I spoke up when I am usually very quiet and, because of this, got better results than I expected.

3. Identify two situations where you missed the chance to turn an opportunity into a success.

4. What caused you to miss the opportunity?

5. *Based on how you answered Number 3, what would you do differently if you faced situations like this again?*

Think about what you did in other situations that made you successful.

Chapter 9
Basking in the Glow

I'm living my life like its golden.

Jill Scott

It's easy to know what it feels like not to succeed. We've all experienced failure. But trying to know what it feels like to succeed in the ways I have been talking about in this book -- to be one of those who has gotten to the other side using the techniques I've described -- is sometimes more difficult to imagine.

The trip is somewhat like crossing a stream while hiking. What does it feel like to reach the far shore? What goes on in the minds of those who have crossed over and conquered the obstacles life placed before them and have made the changes necessary to becoming better than they believed was ever possible?

In this chapter I want to provide a sense of what success feels like and some of the characteristics of those who *bask in the glow* and have felt success.

When people feel positive it radiates to others. It is contagious because others want to also feel that way. Success builds confidence. When I talk with individuals who have used the principles I've discussed here, I find they share a great sense of relief because they have overcome obstacles they did not think it possible to overcome. Confronting and conquering issues that now come before them is also easier because of the confidence they have gained from their earlier successes. They understand, of course, that obstacles will come before them in the future, which is true for everyone, but because of their successes, they feel more confident when approaching these obstacles. Success is now their default position, not failure. The unknown is not nearly as intimidating as before. Let's look at some of the common characteristics of those who bask in the glow.

The Eight Common Elements of Those Who Bask in the Glow

1. They constantly re-evaluate themselves and adjust

It would be a mistake to assume that those who bask in the glow are successful and resting on their laurels and satisfied with their past success. In fact, they are not complacent, nor are they just sitting still. My conception of those who bask in the glow is that they are continually re-evaluating themselves.

They are always making adjustments to be relevant in a constantly changing environment. They believe in change and are adept with surfing the waves of change. On an individual and organization basis, you will see them always monitoring their behavior, getting feedback, testing new programs or behaviors, and moving to higher levels of performance.

If those who *bask in the glow* would remain complacent and self-satisfied, they would not succeed for very long. This is why it is critical for them to continuously evaluate their results and actions. To continuously improve yourself, you also have to believe in continuous learning. One is continuously learning by being receptive to feedback and information.

This does not mean that one is accepting of everything, but it does mean that one needs to consider how this feedback and information can help them improve. It also means being proactive. That is, not waiting for situations to occur and then respond, but anticipating change and preparing accordingly.

2.   *They know when it's now working for them*

Where earlier, an individual would feel the situations they encountered were insurmountable, now they feel optimistic and that their strategies are working for them. They begin to see that achievement earned in one area spills over to other areas.

Warren, an investment banker, was a young man I assisted in changing jobs. He told me that his success at changing jobs led to benefits in both his business relationships, as well as social life. He started to feel confident, and both business partners and women noticed and responded. The melancholy he was in, he said, was driving him into a downward spiral of depression, but since achieving success in his job search, he was now on an upward spiral. "If I can handle this," he said, "I can handle anything."

Mora is a public relations executive. She wanted to move to San Francisco as a way to boost her professional career, but a job opportunity came up in Atlanta instead. Previously, she would not have considered a move to Atlanta, but since she has begun to be more adventurous and receptive to new ideas, Atlanta looks like it could be a good move. Not just because of the job, but because she has family and college colleagues there, and likes the climate. This is a new attitude on her part and it comes from her believing in herself and being willing to take chances that can pay off later.

When you try some things and they work, your confidence gets a boost and you want to try more and more new things. For example, I spoke with Juan, as part of a coaching session, who had a MBA and was laid off from a bank position he held for 10 years since graduating from college. He told me he was continually going on job interviews and getting rejected. His self-confidence was diminishing and he was going emotionally in a downward cycle. He wanted me to review his resume and give him some hints. He did not get the full services of an outplacement firm from his former employer to assist him with his job efforts.

What was missing was a complete picture of what his new vision would be and the distinct skills he had to achieve to reach his vision. With his financial acumen, I recommended he look at other settings where he could apply his skills, such as the government. He got energized and found a job in the pension department of the local municipal government. This turned out to be very positive for him because now he was looking at his background in a very different way and he branded himself as a manager with superb financial analytical skills.

3. They are energized

Let's face it, when you're feeling depressed you want to sleep all day and the last thing you want is to connect with others. When you don't have energy, you run the risk of engaging in negative activities to get an artificial boost to your energy. This may be overeating, alcohol abuse, or drugs. But when feeling well, you are unstoppable, and the downward spiral of depression is completely reversed. There is nothing wrong with seeking more advice from a mental health professional if your depression becomes too overwhelming.

Jane, a social worker, was laid off and felt very despondent. She used food as a way to help cope with her situation. To get out of her out of her bad mood, she decided to visit friends in Florida. While there, to fill her time, she volunteered to work with immigrants.

One thing led to another, as they say, and the organization where she volunteered offered her a job. When she went to Florida, she had no intention of relocating there, nor did she ever imagine herself working for a non-profit. The pay was low compared to what she was receiving before, but so were her expenses. Now, though, she was open to every possibility.

Never has she felt as energized and excited about her work -- and her life -- than she does now. In fact, she started an exercise regimen of going to the gym and swimming. She didn't have this opportunity before. Her exercise regimen required her to stop using food as a panacea and she started to pay greater attention to her diet. She now had a number of very positive things going on her life. Change was happening on a number of different levels and you could see that she was much more optimistic in her outlook.

When you become *better than you believe*, this is almost always the result. And as you become more energized, you accomplish more, which just builds on your success and this generates even more energy. Again, an upward spiral is created.

Several years ago, I studied martial arts with a particular focus on Tai-chi and Aikido. There is a concept in Aikido called Positive Ki, which means energy. We all exhibit energy, but it can be positive or negative. Positive Ki focuses your energy in productive ways. When you focus on Positive Ki, your energy works for you as opposed to against you. You are able to direct it in a manner that will create positive feelings, renew your mind and body, and refresh your spirit. I believe that Positive

Ki is unleashed when you engage in various forms of personal reflection, meditation or prayer. That is why Jane was starting to feel so much better about her choices. She was experiencing the effect of Positive Ki. In sports, many athletes will tell you that they performed well because they were in the "zone." They were able to perform better than they believed and they surpassed their expectations by aligning mind, spirit and body to accomplish great tasks.

4. They exhibit accountability

When feeling successful, you begin to feel more ownership and commitment for your actions. Some people go through life blaming others for what happens to them. They don't take responsibility for their actions; they blame others for holding them back, and blame others for not giving them an opportunity to progress. As you begin to take more responsibility and accountability for your actions, you begin to see that you can influence the outcomes. You are not powerless and a victim of circumstances.

5. They believe in paying it forward

There's an African proverb that says, "In order to get another out of the river, you need to have one foot on the bank." I have a friend who talks about being able to mentor others and to give back to others in the same way others have given to him. Since he left his previous job he has become more optimistic and is positioning himself to be a role model for others, rather than just being primarily and selfishly focused on himself. He has a greater sense of self-empowerment and is more assertive. Now, he can look people in the eye and give them better advice with greater certainty and clarity.

When people feel empowered like this, it is almost contagious. You pass on to others the learning and wisdom that you have gained, and show you want to help others succeed as much as you want to help yourself. This is *"paying it forward."* There are many people who always are looking for someone to mentor them or give them advice. Those who pay it forward seek to mentor and are unselfish with giving advice to others.

In graduate school, some professors were always difficult to talk to after class. They had certain office hours, but you never felt comfortable going into their office asking for advice. On the other hand, one of my professors, Dr. Hackshaw, always had time to talk to students. Whether you took his classes or not, you felt you could go into his office and he would have loads of worldly advice. Even when I graduated from college, I would call upon him and he would provide his wisdom. Probably all of us remember a person like this in our lives. They have a reputation that is memorable and has a lasting impact on our lives.

There is an interesting quiz that highlights this point that is often attributed to Charles Schulz, the syndicated cartoonist and creator of Peanuts. He said name the five wealthiest people in the world. Then name the last five Heisman trophy winners, 10 people who won the Nobel or Pulitzer Prize, and the last six Academy Award winners for Best Film. Usually, we can name only a few of these individuals although they were the best in their field.

Then he asked if people can name the teachers who aided their journey through school, name three friends who helped them through a difficult time, name a few people who made you feel appreciated and special, and name five people you enjoy spending time with. Answering these questions is much easier.

The point is that the ones who matter most in your life are not those with the most credentials, money, or awards. They are simply those who demonstrate that they care the most. This is what the concept of paying it forward is all about.

6. *They are resilient*

When we talk about resilience, we are talking about those people who are able to bounce by after facing adversity. We all face difficult circumstances during certain times in our life that can knock us down, literally and figuratively. However, not everyone is resilient enough to continue to keep going and move their life forward.

7. *They have a future orientation*

Handling challenges in the present becomes easier if you feel the outcomes in the future will be positive. Some people feel their present situation is always going to be negative, which makes it difficult for them to face problems. They are so involved in thinking about their present negative circumstances that they don't think about or plan for a better situation. But they could endure pain in the present if they believe that using certain strategies can create a better future.

Some people who are involved in the present like to complain and get together in groups and talk about how bad things are. They don't strategize to improve their circumstances, but would rather complain and moan about it. Future oriented people are usually thinking about how things can be different tomorrow. They interact with those who also plan and strategize to create a much more positive outlook.

Is the light you see at the end of a tunnel from a train coming to run you over, or an exit to the light and a better situation? Future oriented people can see the light at the end of the tunnel and it is not a train.

Another important characteristic of future oriented people is their ability to delay gratification. It is easy to feel that you have to spend and consume in the present because you are unsure of what tomorrow may bring. Future oriented people are more optimistic and feel they have the ability to reap benefits in the future by not giving in to immediate impulses.

8. *They innately feel they are in the right space*

I know a marketing executive who always values the time

he spends with people. When I spoke to him about what it feels like to bask in the glow, he says it is like feeling you are in the right place, the place you should be, doing the things you should be doing and being with the people you should be with. It is extremely important to seek an environment that supports your values. It's important to find a space that reinforces who you are and what you are trying to do.

Call it instinct. Call it intuition. Those who bask in the glow know they will be successful doing what they are doing, and realize they can use their present situation to create miracles. When they put it all together and think about their present situation, life circumstances, abilities, and challenges, they know they will overcome any issues that confront them. It is human to feel some fear when trying something new or taking risks, but those that reach success do not let their fears prevent them from taking the action needed to reach their goals. As long as they have well designed strategies that include built-in contingency plans to keep them on course, they know they can overcome any issues that may confront them.

Chapter 10
Epilogue

*"Always dream and shoot higher than you know how to.
Don't bother to just be better than your contemporaries
or predecessors. Try to be better than yourself."*

William Faulkner

My goal in this book is to highlight how individuals and organizations can develop strategies for positive change. I have outlined several steps that can be used to facilitate a transition to more effective levels of performance and behavior. Ultimately, it is not a destination, but a journey.

You never get there all at once. It may take several attempts and small steps to get you where you want to be. It is important to take note of your strengths and focus on how to leverage them in different ways.

When you reach a milestone and overcome one of your hurdles, it is important to celebrate those successes. You should take note of the moment and relish what it means in relation to your overall plan. You should not become complacent with what you have accomplished. Instead, strive to continuously improve. Look for the next horizon. Be ready to tackle whatever may arise next.

Finishing this book has been an important step in my own journey. It outlines what I have learned about people and organizations. I share it in the hope that you, the reader, will find value that can improve your life and the lives of others.

Quotes or Commentary

Philip Berry is a talented leader with exceptional business acumen, leadership capability and vision. Philip's global corporate and consulting experience coupled with his engaging style of communication has enabled him to affect change in a multitude of settings.

In "Better Than You Believe," Philip will masterfully guide you through the process of becoming more self aware, identifying your personal "board of directors" and creating an agenda of action leading to more positive personal and professional outcomes.

Eugene Kelly, Director of Global Workplace Initiatives; Colgate Palmolive

"If you have ever dreamed of changing your life or visualized yourself in a new and more fulfilling job, this book is for you. With light piano teacher fingers, Philip A. Berry takes the reader to new levels of creative insight, blending real-life situations with strategic "how-to" advice and practical techniques."

Jay Hershenson, Senior Vice Chancellor for University

Relations and Secretary, Board of Trustees, The City University of New York

Being Better than You Believe' is an excellent tool for mapping out strategies and programs to get more out of life so that you can reach your highest potential. Philip Berry details eight proven strategies of success and he shows you can use them by providing practical examples that everyone can relate to. Philip Berry is an inspirational figure who has helped many people find their way to greater personal fulfillment. I believe that this book can be of benefit to many people as they travel along on life's journey.

Love H. Whelchel, III
Chief Talent Officer
Global Human Resources
Young & Rubicam

Appendix
Living More Values List!

VALUES LIST

1. Abundance

2. Acceptance

3. Accessibility

4. Accomplishment

5. Accuracy

6. Achievement

7. Acknowledgement

8. Activeness

9. Adaptability

10. Adoration

11. Adroitness

12. Adventure

13. Affection

14. Affluence

15. Aggressiveness

16. Agility

17. Alertness

18. Altruism

19. Ambition

20. Amusement

21. Anticipation

22. Appreciation

23. Approachability

24. Articulacy

25. Assertiveness	46. Capability
26. Assurance	47. Care
27. Attentiveness	48. Carefulness
28. Attractiveness	49. Celebrity
29. Audacity	50. Certainty
30. Availability	51. Challenge
31. Awareness	52. Charity
32. Awe	53. Charm
33. Balance	54. Chastity
34. Beauty	55. Cheerfulness
35. Being the best	56. Clarity
36. Belonging	57. Cleanliness
37. Benevolence	58. Clear-mindedness
38. Bliss	59. Cleverness
39. Boldness	60. Closeness
40. Bravery	61. Comfort
41. Brilliance	62. Commitment
42. Buoyancy	63. Compassion
43. Calmness	64. Completion
44. Camaraderie	65. Composure
45. Candor	66. Concentration

67. Confidence	88. Cunning
68. Conformity	89. Curiosity
69. Congruency	90. Daring
70. Connection	91. Decisiveness
71. Consciousness	92. Decorum
72. Consistency	93. Deference
73. Contentment	94. Delight
74. Continuity	95. Dependability
75. Contribution	96. Depth
76. Control	97. Desire
77. Conviction	98. Determination
78. Conviviality	99. Devotion
79. Coolness	100. Devoutness
80. Cooperation	101. Dexterity
81. Cordiality	102. Dignity
82. Correctness	103. Diligence
83. Courage	104. Direction
84. Courtesy	105. Directness
85. Craftiness	106. Discipline
86. Creativity	107. Discovery
87. Credibility	108. Discretion

109. Diversity

110. Dominance

111. Dreaming

112. Drive

113. Duty

114. Dynamism

115. Eagerness

116. Economy

117. Ecstasy

118. Education

119. Effectiveness

120. Efficiency

121. Elation

122. Elegance

123. Empathy

124. Encouragement

125. Endurance

126. Energy

127. Enjoyment

128. Entertainment

129. Enthusiasm

130. Excellence

131. Excitement

132. Exhilaration

133. Expectancy

134. Expediency

135. Experience

136. Expertise

137. Exploration

138. Expressiveness

139. Extravagance

140. Extroversion

141. Exuberance

142. Fairness

143. Faith

144. Fame

145. Family

146. Fascination

147. Fashion

148. Fearlessness

149. Ferocity

150. Fidelity

151. Fierceness

152. Financial independence

153. Firmness

154. Fitness

155. Flexibility

156. Flow

157. Fluency

158. Focus

159. Fortitude

160. Frankness

161. Freedom

162. Friendliness

163. Frugality

164. Fun

165. Gallantry

166. Generosity

167. Gentility

168. Giving

169. Grace

170. Gratitude

171. Gregariousness

172. Growth

173. Guidance

174. Happiness

175. Harmony

176. Health

177. Heart

178. Helpfulness

179. Heroism

180. Holiness

181. Honesty

182. Honor

183. Hopefulness

184. Hospitality

185. Humility

186. Humor

187. Hygiene

188. Imagination

189. Impact

190. Impartiality

191. Independence

192. Industry

193. Ingenuity

194. Inquisitiveness

195. Insightfulness

196. Inspiration

197. Integrity

198. Intelligence

199. Intensity

200. Intimacy

201. Intrepidness

202. Introversion

203. Intuition

204. Intuitiveness

205. Inventiveness

206. Investing

207. Joy

208. Judiciousness

209. Justice

210. Keenness

211. Kindness

212. Knowledge

213. Leadership

214. Learning

215. Liberation

216. Liberty

217. Liveliness

218. Logic

219. Longevity

220. Looking good

221. Love

222. Loyalty

223. Majesty

224. Making a difference

225. Mastery

226. Maturity

227. Meekness

228. Mellowness

229. Meticulousness

230. Mindfulness

231. Modesty

232. Motivation

233. Mysteriousness

234. Nature

235. Neatness

236. Nerve

237. Obedience

238. Open-mindedness

239. Openness

240. Optimism

241. Order

242. Organization

243. Originality

244. Outlandishness

245. Outrageousness

246. Passion

247. Peace

248. Perceptiveness

249. Perfection

250. Perkiness

251. Perseverance

252. Persistence

253. Persuasiveness

254. Philanthropy

255. Piety

256. Playfulness

257. Pleasantness

258. Pleasure

259. Poise

260. Polish

261. Popularity

262. Potency

263. Power

264. Practicality

265. Pragmatism

266. Precision

267. Preparedness

268. Presence

269. Privacy

270. Proactivity

271. Professionalism

272. Prosperity

273. Prudence

274. Punctuality

275. Purity

276. Realism

277. Reason	298. Sacrifice
278. Reasonableness	299. Sagacity
279. Recognition	300. Saintliness
280. Recreation	301. Sanguinity
281. Refinement	302. Satisfaction
282. Reflection	303. Security
283. Relaxation	304. Self-control
284. Reliability	305. Selflessness
285. Religiousness	306. Self-reliance
286. Resilience	307. Sensitivity
287. Resolution	308. Sensuality
288. Resolve	309. Serenity
289. Resourcefulness	310. Service
290. Respect	311. Sexuality
291. Rest	312. Sharing
292. Restraint	313. Shrewdness
293. Reverence	314. Significance
294. Richness	315. Silence
295. Rigor	316. Silliness
296. Ritual	317. Simplicity
297. Sacredness	318. Sincerity

319. Skillfulness	340. Temperance
320. Solidarity	341. Thankfulness
321. Solitude	342. Thoroughness
322. Soundness	343. Thoughtfulness
323. Speed	344. Thrift
324. Spirit	345. Tidiness
325. Spirituality	346. Timeliness
326. Spontaneity	347. Traditionalism
327. Spunk	348. Tranquility
328. Stability	349. Transcendence
329. Stealth	350. Trust
330. Stillness	351. Trustworthiness
331. Strength	352. Truth
332. Structure	353. Understanding
333. Success	354. Unflappability
334. Support	355. Uniqueness
335. Supremacy	356. Unity
336. Surprise	357. Usefulness
337. Sympathy	358. Utility
338. Synergy	359. Valor
339. Teamwork	360. Variety

361. Victory

362. Vigor

363. Virtue

364. Vision

365. Vitality

366. Vivacity

367. Warmth

368. Watchfulness

369. Wealth

370. Willfulness

371. Willingness

372. Winning

373. Wisdom

374. Wittiness

375. Wonder

376. Youthfulness

377. Zeal

Copyright 2008 - Living More, LLC